HOW GAMES GET MADE

HOW GAMES GET MADE

THE STORIES OF THE PEOPLE WHO MAKE AND PLAY THE GAMES WE LOVE

EMMA SCHAALE

NEW DEGREE PRESS

HOW GAMES GET MADE

The Stories of the People Who Make and Play the Games We Love

ISBN   978-1-63676-548-8 *Paperback*

978-1-63676-115-2 *Kindle Ebook*

978-1-63676-116-9 *Ebook*

To Mom, Dad, Gregory

ACKNOWLEDGEMENTS

I'd like to gratefully acknowledge these people for contributing to my Indiegogo crowdsourcing campaign. Without you, I would not have been able to make this book a reality.

Mom, Dad, Grandma, Grandpa, Aunt Saori, Mrs. Leigh, Ms. Smith, Ms. Ryan, Mr. Walker, Ms. Atsuko Takenouchi, Chaim "Jim-San" Hisiger, Professor Joe Loporcaro, Professor Eric Koester, Professor Stephanie Ashenfelder, Grant Dever, Allegra Tennis, Meaghan Moody, Emily Sherwood, Laquanda M. Fields, the Karp family, Chris Pruszynski, Julia Moch, Will Mackay, Hongyu Li, Hank Lasley, May Shin Lyan, Jonah Shafran, Megan Whiskin, Terena Keehn, Kelsea Papaleo, Cindy Gao, Daria Potapova, Daniel Klosowski, Muhammed El-Sayed, Takanori Tanaka, Saori Takahashi, Peter K. Joyce, Keiko Nakayama, Satoko Kiyohara, Mako Tsujimoto, Mary Lester, Udain Tomar, Forrest Shooster, Colleen Kirchoff, Kathryn DeFeo, Sean Janse van Rensburg, Cate Keeney, Yuko Dunham, William Wilson, Suzuki Katsuhiro, Kevin Kirchoff, Nae Hayakawa, Chiyo Higashiyama, Nae Hayakawa, Eriko Isobe, Lynn Schiro, Miyuki Yamada, Fumie Iuchi, Maria Chavarria, Owen Rumiano, Barbara G.

Hindman, Meg McQuillan, Gary Cookhorn, Hideji Nishikawa, Pete Danielsen, Paul Tracy, Robert Mostyn, Masahito Kato, Suzanne S. Katz, Lindsay Cronk, Roxana Bowgen, Sean Baptiste, Lisa Pendse, Rohit Crasta, Gregory Kirchoff, and Liz Kirchoff.

I'd also like acknowledge those who have brought this book to life:

David Cage, Gordon Walton, Dakota Herold, Jan Rigerl, Ian Schreiber, Feargus Urquhart, Sean Baptiste, Lisa Pendse, Ingrid Sanassee, MissKyliee, Spuddy, and Larry Mellon.

Thank you for taking the time to speak with me.

I'd also like to thank those at New Degree Press who helped shape this book: Michael Bailey, John Chancey, Victoria Lei, Gjorgji Pejkovski, and Agata Wawryniuk.

I'd finally like to thank Eric Koester for founding the Creators Institute and Brian Bies at New Degree Press Publishing for increasing accessibility of authorship for students.

CONTENTS

———

INTRODUCTION

———

Today's just another one of those days. Your mother is badgering you about becoming a lawyer or a doctor. "Or maybe sticking with finance is the way to go," she suggests. Your father warns you about the grades for your calculus class, in which you're dangerously close to falling past a C minus. You know, the usual. Giving lifeless nods and noncommittal answers in response, you wander back to your bedroom.

Ah, your bedroom. Your safe haven. Your small paradise within the grueling desert of daily life. Your gaming console of choice rests under the TV your parents got for you after several years of begging, and your headset that promises professional-quality sound rests in its charging stand. You grab the controller, put on your headset, and pick up the bag of snacks you were eating before you headed downstairs for dinner. Popping in your favorite game, you check the time. Sweet. It's 8 p.m. on a Friday, and the weekend's ahead of you. After five weekdays of exhausting work, relaxing with some games will be nice for a change.

You might enjoy playing games. In fact, you might spend more time gaming than doing "actual" work. But what if your actual work was working within the gaming industry?

This thought didn't even occur to me until I took my first video game development course in college, at age twenty. Despite the ridiculous number of hours I'd spent playing and watching games, I didn't realize I could make the stuff until far later.

I originally went to college to study biology and astronomy. Before the end of my first semester, that became photography, another hobby of mine. However, finding that too restrictive of a medium to express what I wanted, video game development became my salvation after two years of unrelated classes.

Video games constitute a large class of software. From *Candy Crush* (2012), the mobile smash hit, to *Counter Strike: Global Offensive* (2012), one of the most popular online multiplayer games, to *Nancy Drew: Interactive Mysteries* (1998), a kids' education game, when I discuss video game development, I mean it as an all-encompassing term. It includes the games your eighty-year-old grandmother plays on her iPad as well as the games that eighteen-year-old eSports players engage in.

Maybe you picked up this book because you like playing video games, or you've never considered "making games" as a professional career path. Or maybe you're reading it because you want to work in the game industry but are nervous on how to do so. Or maybe you already work in the industry and wanted to hear some other perspectives. Perhaps you even considered becoming a Twitch streamer to play games in front of an audience, but you have no idea where to begin.

I'm here to share with you the ins and outs of the gaming industry and answer questions, such as:

- How, exactly, do people get into the gaming industry?
- What does "working in the industry" even mean?
- How do I become an industry leader?
- What is it like to build your own business in this industry?

With those questions in mind, I should note the video game industry is unique. It's volatile and often requires overtime, and most of the people who work in it do so for passion rather than career stability or pay. The industry is so new that finding a clear-cut base pay rate for any single role is difficult. Your hours and pay are so dependent upon the work culture of the company, your job, and the progression of the developing project that it is almost impossible to give a clear answer.

Take, for example, the job position of 2-D/2-D Concept artist. For a junior/mid-level role, here are the pay rates I can find at a quick glance, including the artists' location and company:

- Roxie Vizcarra, @roxination: $75,000 in 2009 working at Rockstar Games in New York City[1]
- Marc Brunet, @bluefley: $41,000 (CAD) in 2007 working at Behavior Interactive in unknown location[2]

---

1   Roxie Vizcarra, Twitter Post, June 10, 2020, 1:48 p.m.

2   Marc Brunet, Twitter Post, June 8, 2020, 1:30 a.m.

- Anisa Sanusi, @studioanisa: $19,000 in 2013 working at unknown company in North England[3]

However, individuals working in the game development industry have attempted to give some clarity on social media platforms like Twitter. I highly recommend you do your own investigating on hashtags like #gamedevpaidme, a hashtag that came about in June 2020 as a means of finding the hours, work culture, and pay rate of companies, geographic locations, or careers you may want to pursue. The answers are so varied that I could not sum them up in a concise, accurate way in this book.

Think about the sacrifices a doctor must make for their career. An additional four years of medical school combined with several hundred thousands of dollars of debt, and yet another three to five years of residency where they are paid little over minimum wage to work as a wage slave for hospitals, coupled with the fear of being sued for malpractice and losing their license when they finally "get the job." Yet they endure grueling conditions for the prestige, the money, or passion. In the same way, those who work in the game industry do so for one of two reasons: the money or the passion. It's certainly not the prestige, and it's rarely the money.

Every person I interviewed for this book mentioned how this was a pursuit of passion more than anything. In spite of career and financial uncertainty, they were willing to do that because they were able to realize a creative idea they could not have otherwise in another medium.

---

3   Anisa Sanusi, Twitter Post, June 7, 2020, 4:29 p.m.

If I've learned one thing, it's that sacrifice and passion are required. No, you don't have to cut off all ties from your family or never hang out with your friends ever again. And you certainly don't have to stay up until 4 a.m. every night working—in fact, as somebody who regularly sleeps by 10 p.m. and wakes up by 7 a.m., I'd highly advise against that. But you might have to turn down a get together or two in order to get those thousand words done for the day or cut into your hour of relaxation before sleep to finish rendering a scene. And I'll say that it'd be damn difficult to do this without sacrifice and passion.

The video game industry still has a perception of being "immature" or "childish." I often hesitate when bringing up my career path to "adults" when they ask me what I do, and the pitiful, confused answer I seem to receive from an unfortunate majority is a testament to that fact. That is an unbecoming way to refer to the enormous business model that governs the game industry. Here are just a couple of the types of careers required to have a decently successful company:

- Game development requires level designers, programmers, UI/UX developers, and quality assurance testers.
- Music and sound production requires audio engineers, music composers, and often live, professional musicians in order to achieve studio-quality sound.
- Art requires concept artists, illustrators and/or animators, storyboard artists, and technical artists.
- Marketing requires unique relationships with online 'influencers,' on top of traditional advertising marketing on TV or in shows.

- Business-side requires management of all of these projects constantly shifting priority, funding, and expenses.

Most importantly, remember the software and hardware used by each of these roles are constantly upgrading to realize the true complexity of the interconnected nature of a gaming company. Take, for example, the two most popular video game development engines: Unreal Engine 4, created by Epic Games, and Unity, created by Unity Technologies. Both are similar in scope, and the two tech giants are constantly releasing large updates every couple of months with new features, trying to outdo the other.

This rapid updating of equipment is simply unheard of in other industries, like the film industry, for example. You wouldn't expect, as a cinematographer, that instead of measuring depth of field using aperture, you're now using something called "aperture_version1.14.5," which is a bit more economically efficient but requires you to learn more about the optics of apertures to be able to use it. And imagine that happening multiple times a year.

Such constantly improving and competing software companies are an example of what makes the game industry has one of the most complex business models that reaps the rewards from the seeds it sows: it made $43.4 billion in sales in the US in 2018, growing 18 percent from the year previous.[4] This revenue far outpaces that of the film industry in 2017, which commands $31 billion of the market share. The film industry

---

4   "U.S. Video Game Sales Reach Record-Breaking $43.4 Billion in 2018," Entertainment Software Association, 2020.

also projects to grow only 2 percent a year through 2022.[5] The video game industry is a rapidly growing industry that will continue to grow in the future.

In this book, we will be exploring the different perspectives of those working within the industry. We will follow:

- Feargus Urquhart, who started off as an engineering major at University of California, Riverside, and ended up as CEO of Obsidian Entertainment with the famous *Fallout* series under his belt.
- Ingrid Sanassee, Motion Kit director at Quantic Dream, and how she went from having no access to computers on Mauritius, a tropical island off the coast of Madagascar where she grew up, to ending up in Paris, France, as a Motion Kit lead at Quantic Dream.
- Sean Baptiste, influencer manager at Bethesda, and how he went from having a partially completed degree, no job, and brain tumor, to working with top online personalities like Markiplier and T-Pain in order to market Bethesda's top franchises.

...and many, many more.

Each of these stories shares a perspective of how you can get your foot in the door. Whether you find your way into a large development or publishing company, or start up your own indie video game company, it's a way of finding a way to work doing what you love.

---

5   "Movie & Video Production Industry in the US - Market Research Report," IBISWorld, July 14, 2020.

What drew me to creating video games was ultimately my love not just for playing games, but the game itself as a whole: the story, the graphics, the characters, the music, and the art. Realizing that I could have the satisfaction of making them myself was a game changer. I've thrown myself into the various classes with more gusto than I have any of my classes before. 3-D animation and modeling, 2-D pixel art and animation, music composition for games, audio integration, story writing, and cut-scene cinematography have permeated my life for the past three years. I've created two games and am now working on my third.

Working on game development is one of the most rewarding challenges I have taken on. Engines, software, and hardware are constantly shifting; teammates come up with new, innovative ideas to solve a long-standing problem; crafting stories, music, art, and game design all to maximize narrative impact. It has been rewarding so far, and I hope I can only continue from here.

When I started writing this book, I knew I wanted to create a book relating to games or content creation (again, related to games), but I didn't know *what,* exactly, to write about. Luckily, books like *Blood, Sweat, and Pixels: The Triumphant, Turbulent Stories Behind How Video Games Are Made* by Jason Schreier provided an example of how I could contact game developers myself and create stories out of their lives.

Through my research, I had the immense opportunity to network with other game developers like myself, meeting people I could not have imagined speaking to as a teenager playing games in my bedroom. They have given me perspective and fueled my passion for the industry.

Instead of focusing on just game development, I wanted to paint a larger picture of everybody involved in the game industry, whether it be the Twitch streamers who informally help 'sell' the games, the business managers who have to keep track of the finances of every branch of the studio, or the animators who make the characters blossom to life on screen. I didn't want to hear from just the programmers or business executives. I wanted the whole picture.

This book will ignite in you a passion about the video game development industry, regardless of if you plan to work in it professionally. It will help you realize the level of intricacy required in collaboration, networking, and communication. You will learn that so much of this industry is driven by passion, as it is inherent to the very nature of the work. It will leave you wanting to join in.

PART 1

GAME INDUSTRY LEADERS

CHAPTER 1

BREAKING
CONVENTIONS

——

"We try to [have the best of both worlds], with games that try to tell a story, to carry meaning, and where violence isn't the core activity. Most of all, we try to create an emotion, to make players live something strong and unique, which remains an ambitious challenge in a video game."[6]

—DAVID CAGE

Leaders do not come from nowhere. They, like the rest of us, started from somewhere—whether that somewhere was as a junior-level employee or mid-level executive. I'd like to

---

6   Adnan Riaz, "David Cage: 'We're Working on Something Very Exciting,'" GamerHeadlines, November 28, 2014, distributed by The Internet Archive Wayback Machine.

introduce you to the paths many industry leaders took to achieve the positions they have today.

David Cage, a French musician with a passion for composing for film and games, didn't know he would enter the game industry. Originally a classical pianist, Cage started a music career around age fourteen in 1983 by sampling music digitally for clients around Germany and Switzerland.[7]

Eventually, he found he wanted to focus on creating musical pieces for film, television, and games. He moved out of Mulhouse, France, to Montparnasse in Paris to buy his own production studio, "Totem Interactive," when he was a young adult. He sampled for games including *Super Dany* (1994) and *Cheese Cat-Astrophe* (1995).[8]

Cage made a decent living as a freelance music composer for various mediums. In his free time, he played games on the Atari, Nintendo Entertainment System (NES), and Super Nintendo Entertainment System (SNES). He also wrote for fun. One day, he thought: "I want to create a game I want to play."

"I [want] to create a city...there'll be a crowd, and it'll be science fiction, and you'd be able to go wherever you want, whenever you want, and you'd be able to enter all buildings... you could fight," he said.[9] Coworker programmers and com-

---

7   Giuseppe Nelva, "Quantic Dream's David Cage Talks About His Games, His Career and the PS4: It Allows to 'Go Even Further,'" DualSHOCK-ERS, January 4, 2015.

8   Ibid.

9   Ibid.

posers at video game development companies he'd worked for said making such a game in 3-D would be impossible. Still, he managed to convince some friends to work with him to make his idea a reality.

The word "start-up" didn't even exist at this time. The video game industry was highly volatile in the late 1990s, and with companies transitioning from 2-D to 3-D, growth stagnated as its target audience was mostly young- to middle-aged men who were growing out of 'childish' video games. This was an era where gaming company giants like Sony, Sega, and Nintendo were harsh rivals that would pretty much use any means possible to outsmart their competitors. And to convince a group of friends to work on a fresh, new video game idea without the backing of a publisher was a terrifying prospect. Yet Cage pulled it off.

In the late '90s, they developed a game prototype for the Play-Station (PS) console that worked. They were convinced the PlayStation would be the "next big thing." The prototype had a main character that could run around a city environment in real-time 3-D. "Real-time at [that time] was like a miracle," Cage described to me during our interview. Real-time was even more impressive considering it was not an official company creating such a project, but a group of friends who had worked in the industry.

When they rang up publishers in Europe in the late 1990s and showed them their demo, though, publishers simply responded to their prototype with, "Not bad, [but] the Play-Station is a fad" (infuriatingly enough, the PlayStation went on to become the fifth best-selling console of all time, selling over 100 million units).[10] So Cage went to the United States, hoping for a more open-minded reception. The reaction of the publishers was the same there, too, but they had advice for Cage: "Make PC (personal computer) stuff."

Cage returned to France, dejected yet determined. If he had to make a PC demo to prove that his ideas were valid, he would. But he realized it would be difficult to keep working at the slow pace they had been working at to create an entirely new demo for the PC. He came up with the next best solution: he'd quit his music day job, pay his friends with his own money, and form his very own video game studio.

"Let's give ourselves six months, full-time, working our asses off, with a five or six-man team…I'm gonna buy PCs, I'm gonna buy desks, I'm gonna pay you for six months," Cage told his friends. "After six months, we either have a prototype and bingo, we sell it, we start a company, and it's great, or we don't have a prototype, we stop everything, and everybody goes back to what they were doing before."[11]

A few of his friends declined. They had safe positions at their respective jobs (many of whom worked at Cryo Interactive, which would ironically go defunct in 2002). But Cage had four people to work with on his team.

---

10   "Cumulative Production Shipments of Hardware (Until March 2007)," Sony Computer Entertainment Inc., accessed August 19, 2020, distributed by The Internet Archive Wayback Machine.

11   Nelva, "Quantic Dream's David Cage," 2015.

They worked in a fifteen-square-meter soundproof studio. They'd put in an average of twelve to fifteen work hours a day. For game development, they started by creating a 3-D engine from scratch for the PC, using video graphics cards from 3dfx Interactive, a company specializing in 3-D computer chips. They also worked with a motion capture company to incorporate a scanned picture of a man's face onto a 3D model in the game, one of the first in history.

After they finished working on their second prototype, the team called up video game publishers by phone from a directory. Cage managed to land several appointments in London.

One of the publishers he showed his game demo to was Eidos Interactive, also the publisher of *Tomb Raider* (1996), a hugely popular game that went on to sell over seven million units globally.[12]

Cage showed the agent his game demo, who insisted he sign a contract on the spot. "I have to show [the contract] to [my lawyer]," Cage tried to argue.[13] "No, no, you [don't need] a lawyer," the man replied. "But [we have] to talk money..." Cage also tried to point out. "No, no, it's okay, tell me what you want and you'll have it. Listen. You'll be here tomorrow morning. Our lawyer's working, he's preparing your contract, come here tomorrow morning and you'll have it."

12 Chris Glover, "Eidos Celebrates with Lara Croft Tomb Raider: Anniversary," Sci Entertainment Group, March 11, 2006, distributed by the Internet Archive Wayback Machine.

13 Ibid.

"Perhaps he was afraid I'd run away or something," Cage said.[14] He recalls walking out of his meeting, and on the street was a chauffeur waiting for him besides a car that took him to a five-star hotel in London. Cage had never been in a five-star hotel before. The chauffeur even asked Cage if he'd like to meet Arsène Wenger, the French coach of Arsenal, a famous French football team—all as a way to convince him to stick with Eidos, who had seen Cage's potential and leapt on it.

The next day, Cage returned to sign the contract. As had been promised, the contract was ready, along with a French translation of it, as well as a lawyer and a translator. Once the contract was signed and Cage had been promised a fairly large sum of money to create his game with his team (of whom he hadn't even informed yet about the deal, since there was no such thing as the Internet or cell phones yet), Cage returned to his friends at the train station. Once he told them about the deal, they all celebrated.

FUN FACTS:
Favorite Games: Inside (2016), *FIFA* series (1993-)
Companies Worked: Quantic Dream
Game He'd Create with Infinite Resources: *"I have the feeling that I always had the time and resources that I needed to make the games that I wanted. [It's] a very fortunate position."*

---

14   Ibid.

The one important part of the deal, though, was they had to start within a month. Cage didn't even have an official office or employees. They first had to create the studio name; they came up with "Quantic Dream." They bought tables, computers, and even network cables. "You mean everything [has] to be linked?" Cage recalls asking wearily.[15] They also interviewed, hiring folks to work for them. Quantic Dream now had forty employees in total whom Cage had to manage.

Working on the game was difficult. They were a ragtag group of employees working in 3-D, creating a story with combat, adventure, sci-fi, and a complicated story to go along with it. Often, Cage slept under his desk in his office for days in a row just to get extra work done.

"It [was] a lot of personal sacrifices," Cage described to me about this time period. "Just running a company and being in the position of being the guy who needs to think about everything and...provide support and help and ideas for everyone, is time-demanding."

Their first game was ambitious in many ways, and the fact that David Bowie, one of the most influential musicians of the twentieth century, composed the original soundtrack and even starred in the game, was a testament to this fact. This was something unheard of at the time. An actual musician composing a song for a *video game*? *David Bowie*? It would have been ludicrous to tell someone on the streets at the time. Even asking a present-day musician to compose an entire soundtrack for a game *and* star in it is almost preposterous.

---

15   Ibid.

Cage initially wanted Bowie to musically portray the story as the game appeared: cold, emotionless, futuristic. However, Bowie took a different approach. "Your image is already saying [what you want it to say]," Bowie explained, saying the music wouldn't make any contribution to the game if it simply mimicked it. Instead, Bowie wanted to add more depth to the story through music that told a different story than what was actually on the screen. "He came with acoustic music, guitars, drums, vocals," Cage described, "which took the complete opposite view of the visual universe we were trying to depict."[16]

This was something that Cage hadn't considered about his game before: emotions of the story. Of course, it might make sense that a renowned musician would mention a thing or two about the emotional qualities of any type of storytelling. Bowie was innovative enough to view video games and songs both as platforms for conveying emotion. Still, Cage admitted, "[Bowie] talked about [emotions] before I did."[17]

The game, *Nomad Soul: Omikron* (1999), was a decent success, selling just over six hundred thousand copies.[18] However, the development of the game had been demanding for Cage and his team. Relationships with Eidos deteriorated due to the stress Cage and his team experienced. The game itself was highly ambitious, pushing boundaries both technically and creatively. By moving so far ahead of what the industry had

16   Ibid.

17   Ibid.

18   Ellie Gibson, "Quantic Dream Considers Omikron II," *Eurogamer*, Gamer Network Limited, March 17, 2005.

seen or come to expect, the final product was perhaps too far ahead of its time.

Still, the most important thing to come of *Nomad Soul: Omikron* was Cage's desire to go further: to trigger emotions, to tell stories to an audience—and not just a traditional story with a start and an end. He wanted his audience, his players, to have control over the characters' choices in the story.

Luckily, the game wasn't a flop. Quantic Dream had collaborated with David Bowie, after all. And the team still had enough momentum and capital to work on the next project— this time with Atari, Inc. as the publisher.

Their second game, *Fahrenheit,* released in 2005 as another sci-fi thriller with cops and romance and murder, this time with better graphics, better plot organization, and generally better cohesion. Quantic Dream had seventy-five people working on the game.

Toward the end of development, though, Cage became dejected. He feared it would be the last game he'd get to work on. It had a sci-fi plot again with conspiracies and a potential worldwide disaster. Maybe it was too outlandish or too stereotypical.

The sales numbers came as a shock. Moving over one million units, it was named "best adventure game of 2005" by *PC Gamer* and *IGN.*[19] The studio caught international attention.

---

19   "Best Adventure Game - Indigo Prophecy," Best of IGN, IGN Entertainment, 2006, distributed by The Internet Archive Wayback Machine.

Before *Fahrenheit*, Quantic Dream was unknown. "Quantic what?" publishers would say. After shipping *Fahrenheit*, though, their phone rang off the hook. "We saw *Fahrenheit*. Extraordinary. We want to know how we can convince you to work together," they would offer. For the plot, branching storyline, and advanced 3-D character models, publishers were clawing at Quantic Dream's door to be able to work with them.[20]

The game had three different endings based upon the player's choices. Cage was just beginning to realize the potential of games with different plot lines based on the player's decisions. Still, Cage hadn't *really* tapped into what he wanted most. He wanted a truly branching narrative that provoked emotions from the player.

In order to explain this, let me bring up the example of movies again. Movies are entirely linear. They have a one-track storyline the audience has no control over. Horror film movie-goer culture is rife with criticisms of the way actors act in film scenes; rom-com movie-goer culture is rife with criticisms of over-dramatic portrayals of relationships. Either way, the audience member does not have the ability to control the behavior of the actors in the movie.

Cage wanted to change that in video games. He wanted to be able to continue the story past "Game Over." He wanted to see how the world would continue, even with the loss of main characters.

---

20   Nelva, "Quantic Dream's David Cage," 2015.

Cage told me about a time he was in a mall with his son and lost track of him. He was terrified at the idea of not finding his son again. "I wanted to write a story about this moment and this emotion that I felt," he said. Still, he struggled to wrap his mind around the idea of writing for a video game in the same way a writer would for film or a book.

Films and books can be deeply emotional and gut-wrenching and can tread on controversial topics, but games are associated with being silly, childish, and immature. Remember, this was the mid-2000s. Games were supposed to have blood and violence and superheroes, not comment on sensitive cultural and social issues.

Cage stopped and thought, "Wait a second, what am I saying about my medium? Am I saying that it's not equal to films or literature?" He wanted to convey emotions with moral choices that hadn't been done before. "I thought, 'Okay, let's try it.'"

As the team at Quantic Dream started to work on their third game, they grew from seventy-five to 110. Cage wrote a two-thousand-page script for the story. This time, the story just seemed to click. It wasn't the knowledge that he had eyes on his work now or that his company was growing. It was the fact that he could talk about something that touched him. This "something" was that moment he lost his son in the mall.

Heavy Rain, Quantic Dream's third game, released in 2010. The game features cops and serial killers and, of course, a father who has lost his son. The game places heavy focus on the player's choices and emotions. Unlike *Fahrenheit* and

Nomad Soul: Omikron, which focus more on action and fighting, *Heavy Rain* has little to no actual "combat."

Cage gave *Heavy Rain* a pre-release sales estimate of two hundred thousand to three hundred thousand. The game sold over one million copies within five weeks.[21] It won many awards, including the British Academy Video Games Awards (2011) for Technical Innovation, Original Music, and Story and the Japan Game Awards (2010) for Game Design.[22] It sent shockwaves throughout the gaming world as to *what*, exactly, a game could be.

"It has been hugely gratifying to see the positive response that *Heavy Rain* has received from gamers," Cage said in a statement after the game was released.[23] "It shows us that it is possible to create games that break [from] convention, games that seek to tell complex stories, and games that can inspire unexpected emotions in players."

For me, too, *Heavy Rain* was an incredible experience. It was the first Quantic Dream game I ever played. The facial models and expressions astounded me. And the concept that a game didn't have to be about leveling up and defeating the

---

21   Mike Sharkey, "Heavy Rain Passes the Million Sales Marker," GameSpy, April 13, 2010.

22   "2011 Winners & Nominees," BAFTA, British Academy of Film and Television Arts, February 15, 2011; "Heavy Rain Awarded during the Japan Games Awards," Quantic Dream, September 18, 2010, distributed by The Internet Archive Wayback Machine.

23   Alex Pavey, "Heavy Rain Hits 1 Million Sales," PlayStation Blog, April 13, 2010.

"bad guys" changed my perception of the gaming medium. It held more potential than the classical print and film mediums, I thought. Most of all, the fact that I could make choices in the game that could change the ending blew my mind.

Cage has continued to work on successful games with that mechanic. In 2013, Quantic Dream released *Beyond: Two Souls*, a game featuring an even more dramatic story (this time, *with* government conspiracies). Reviews were mixed, but sales were stellar yet again. The game sold one million copies worldwide during its first three months of availability.[24]

Quantic Dream's most recent game, *Detroit: Become Human* (2018), has perhaps been the highest regarded, both commercially and by critics, selling over three million copies in its first eight months of release.[25] It was technically innovative in using motion capture to record actors' expressions. The soundtrack, composed by three separate composers for the three main characters, beautifully matches every character's personality.

"It's a fantasy I had for years and years," Cage said about the soundtrack. The idea came up during the production of *Fahrenheit*, but they couldn't do it then. They couldn't do it for *Heavy Rain,* either, which also features multiple main characters. When he got to the development of *Detroit:*

24 David Hinkle, "Beyond: Two Souls Sales Topped 1 Million in 2013," Engadget, January 10, 2014.

25 Dean Takahashi, "Why Netease and Quantic Dream Are Teaming up for Games on Multiple Platforms," VentureBeat, January 29, 2019.

Become Human, though, Cage thought he'd never do it if he didn't manage to get it done for this game.

The script for *Detroit: Become Human* also consisted of over four thousand pages. What's more impressive than the number, though, is the fact that Cage considers all aspects of game design before writing the story.

"What I tried to do was not to have story on one side, mechanics on the other," Cage said about writing the script with the game design in mind. "You need the two to work together… Otherwise, it will feel artificial." By doing so, Cage was able to create over forty endings to the game.

David Cage has proved time and time again the ingenuity of thinking outside the box and breaking conventions within the game industry. By making sacrifices in his personal life to work on projects that were deemed "impossible" by professionals in the field he wasn't yet a part of, he was able to work past the criticism to become a better storyteller and game developer. It's important to reflect that view upon ourselves to realize how we may be holding ourselves back from even considering joining the game industry, let alone working on a game ourselves.

CHAPTER 2

FOR THE LOVE
OF DEATH

———

"[Dark Souls] focuses a lot on death, but what is death? What does it look like? What does death mean in this world? What does it mean to live and to die? That is something we discussed very closely. The story is about a fire in the world, a symbol of both living and death. The fire is what brought death to Dark Souls' world, but also the only hope for life. Demons, chaos, dragons, all of them are different incarnations and representations of our idea of death in Dark Souls."[26]

—HIDETAKA MIYAZAKI

---

26   Keza MacDonald, "The Mind Behind Dark Souls," IGN, January 12, 2018.

During a snowstorm on a busy, steep road in Japan, Hidetaka Miyazaki realized his car was stuck—his, along with all of the cars ahead of and behind him. The sleet on the road had grown thick, causing the vehicles to lose traction. Miyazaki wouldn't be able to make it home.

Suddenly, he felt his car lurch forward. The car behind his had driven into him. When he looked back, he could see all the cars piling up to form a line in an effort to creep up the hill.

With the support of strangers, Miyazaki managed to get home safely. The only thing that bothered him, though, was not being able to thank any of the people in the other cars who had helped him. "On the way back home, I wondered whether the last person in the line had made it home," he thought. Had he met those individuals in different contexts, would he have been friends or foes with them? "I would probably never meet the people who had helped me. Oddly, that incident will probably linger in my heart for a long time. Simply because it's fleeting."[27]

This attitude and approach to life is what Miyazaki brings to his game development process. Part-designer, part-philosopher, his approach to creating games is unusual—just like the origins of where he comes from.

Hidetaka Miyazaki didn't start off as a rich man by any means. He grew up poor in a city called Shizuoka, one hundred miles south of Tokyo, Japan. Young Miyazaki would

27   Keza MacDonald, "Souls Survivor," *Eurogamer*, May 28, 2010.

often visit his local library to find stories he could read to entertain himself for free.

"It was a rich reading experience...I found so much joy in those stories," Miyazaki said in a rare profile interview with *The Guardian*.[28] The Japanese don't often do profile interviews: it's considered a bit arrogant to consider yourself important enough to be interviewed, especially if the questions asked concern your life before you became famous. Sometimes the books he read were in English, and he'd use his imagination to fill in gaps in the plot that he did not understand.

Miyazaki also lacked passion as a child. "Unlike most kids in Japan, I didn't have a dream," he described.[29] Without motivation to drive him toward a particular career, he moved through life aimlessly.

By the time Miyazaki was an adult, he was just another student studying the social sciences at Keio University—albeit a prestigious university. Though he contemplated game development during his college years, he ended up becoming just your average businessman in Japan: a "salaryman," as it's called in Japanese culture. He worked at the American IT company Oracle Corporation, based in Japan. He balanced numbers and money in accounts dispassionately but without complaint.

---

28 Simon Parkin, "Bloodborne Creator Hidetaka Miyazaki: 'I Didn't Have a Dream. I Wasn't Ambitious,'" *The Guardian*, March 31, 2015.

29 Ibid.

As the years carried on, his job wore down on him. He was approaching his late twenties, and his position at Oracle was looking more like a dead-end job without a chance at promotion. In Japan, you traditionally stick with one company from the moment you're hired out of college; missing opportunities of promotions is equivalent to being told you'll be a deadbeat for the rest of your life.

But then Miyazaki began to play some games with friends again in his late twenties. They played *Ico* (2001), a fantastical escape adventure game, making their way through castles from ghastly villains. And Miyazaki realized: "I wanted to make one myself."[30] He loved the theme of fantasy, how far away from our world the game seemed. He wanted to create something similar.

FUN FACTS:
Games He's Worked On: *Dark Souls* (2011), *Demon's Souls* (2009)
Companies Worked: FromSoftware, Inc.
Favorite Games: *Dungeons & Dragons* (1974-)[31]

The only problem with finding a new job was that he'd spent nearly a comfortable decade at his IT job: at the time, being twenty-nine years old, he was too old to apply for graduate studies in game development. On top of that, for Miyazaki

---

30   Ibid.

31   Marty Sliva, "Inside the Mind of Bloodborne and Dark Souls' Creator - IGN First," IGN, January 12, 2018.

to consider leaving a comfortable, stable IT job in Japan was unheard of.

Still, Miyazaki applied for jobs exclusively in the game development industry, hoping anywhere would take him. Eventually, after some searching, Miyazaki happened upon FromSoftware, Inc., a game company.[32] He began in 2004 as a programmer.

The first project he worked on was *Armored Core: Last Raven* (2005), a robot action game series. He joined in the midst of its development. After he completed his work on that project, he was promoted to main planner for *Armored Core 4* (2006), and then again to director during that project.[33] When it released in December of 2006, it wasn't a disaster, but it wasn't a success either: the game received mixed reviews from Famitsu (a 7.8/10) and Game Informer (a 6.5/10).[34], [35]

The second project Miyazaki worked on, though, was *Demon's Souls*, a fantasy-action RPG that released in 2009 for the PS3 that promised more challenge than the average fantasy RPG. The publisher for *Demon's Souls* was Sony Computer Entertainment, another company in Japan.

32 Ibid.

33 "Armored Core 4," MobyGames, Blue Flame Labs, accessed August 21, 2020.

34 Famitsu, "アーマード・コア4のレビュー・評価・感想 [Armored Core 4 Review]," Kadokawa Game Linkage Inc., accessed August 21, 2020.

35 Bryan Vore, "Core Mech Values," Game Informer, accessed August 21, 2020, distributed by The Internet Archive Wayback Machine.

"*Demon's Souls* wasn't doing well…the project had problems and the team had been unable to create a compelling prototype," Miyazaki said. "But when I heard it was a fantasy-action RPG, I was excited. I figured I could find a way to take control of the game…If my ideas failed, nobody would care—it was already a failure."[36] With this ironically fatalistic and opportunistic mindset, similar to that which he experienced during the snowstorm, Miyazaki set to work on the game.

Because of the expectations of failure, Miyazaki felt comfortable bringing his own perspective onto the project; he didn't feel he had to adhere to a strict set of standards. And being promoted to director of the project from early on, he was free to do what he wanted. "We wanted to bring back the elements of classic RPGs to the PS3 with *Demon's Souls*," Miyazaki explained in an interview with 4Gamer, a Japanese gaming news site.[37] "Replicating the feeling of attainment when completing a level, or when making a discovery, was important to us."

Demon's Souls was supposed to represent a game at its basic fundamentals: the trial-and-error that games "used to have" in the fantasy games in the '80s and '90s, such as the *Dragon Quest* (1986-) and *Final Fantasy* (1987-) series. "While the game was still [in] development, we weren't being fully understood and it was very difficult for us," said Miyazaki

---

36   Simon Parkin, "Bloodborne Creator."

37   Mafia, Kajita, "なぜいまマゾゲーなの？ ゲーマーの間で評判の"即死ゲー"「Demon's Souls」（デモンズソウル）開発者インタビュー [Why a masochistic game? Interview with 'Demon's Souls' 'sudden death game' popular among gamers]," 4gamer, March 19, 2013.

in an interview with *Eurogamer*. "We weren't interested in following any trends."[38]

What Miyazaki and FromSoftware wanted to do was bring about a sense of *accomplishment* to the player, not necessarily make the game "difficult." Miyazaki notes that "'difficulty' is just one way to offer an intense sense of accomplishment."[39]

FromSoftware knew this would cause problems with Sony. Because Sony was a large company that catered to a large audience, they would want to make sure the game was more "playable," or friendlier to the average player. And in the late 2000s that *Demon's Souls* was going to be released in, pure difficulty of a video game was not something that was to be celebrated as much as, perhaps, a decade or two ago. Games were now player-friendly—they held your hand when they needed to. They made sure you could win. And that made Miyazaki afraid of emphasizing just how "difficult" *Demon's Souls* would be.

Naturally, Miyazaki kept quiet about the game's actual difficulty at pitch meetings with Sony. They wouldn't go into the specifics of the death mechanics of the game, instead talking about the topic as vaguely as they could.

Even their producer at Sony, Takeshi Kaji, agreed that if Miyazaki were too honest about the death system to the marketing department, the publishing company would force

38   Keza MacDonald, "Souls Survivor."

39   Phil Kollar, "Demon's Souls Director Discusses Difficulty, Sequels, and More," Game Informer, November 5, 2009.

them to scrap the game. "So that's why we had to be a bit sneaky about it," Miyazaki explained.[40]

Despite Miyazaki's efforts, *Demon's Souls* received a disastrous preview at the *Tokyo Game Show* of October 2008. With just four months left until release, the demo could barely get through the opening sequence without crashing. Unfortunately, the technical issues prevented players from focusing on the meat of the game: its difficulty. The game only came together very late in development; and even then, it suffered frame rate issues.[41]

Even Sony's president, Shuhei Yoshida, called it, "Crap...an unbelievably bad game."[42] Yoshida himself couldn't get past the introductory area after two hours of playing the game. In a gaming world where demos were supposed to be relatively easy, *Demon's Souls* was an antithesis to that. This fact prevented Yoshida from appreciating what the game was all about: difficulty.

Fast forward to February 2009. In the first week of release, *Demon's Souls* sold 39,589 units in its debut week, trailing behind *Tales of the World Radiant Mythology 2* (the highest selling game that week) by just 5,000 in total copies sold.[43] *Dengeki*, a Japanese game-reviewing magazine, gave

---

40   Keza MacDonald, "The Mind Behind."

41   Jim Reilly, "Sony Talks the Last Guardian, Demon's Souls, and the Vita Launch," Game Informer, February 10, 2012.

42   Ibid.

43   John Tanaka, "Tales of the World Remains at Top in Japan," IGN, June 15, 2012.

the game a 350/400, saying "fans of old-school games will shed tears of joy."[44] In fact, *Demon's Souls* had a 95 percent sales rate, meaning it was almost sold out everywhere.[45] Still, Sony considered these sales numbers slow. They had expected much more units to be sold. So, they decided against porting the game overseas.

Slowly though, things began to change. Despite not having invested much into a marketing campaign (or perhaps due to the fact, causing initial slow sales), the game spread via word of mouth. Its sheer difficulty earned notoriety and respect among gamers, who wanted to complete the game just for the sense of accomplishment it gave. By December 2009, *Demon's Souls* had sold over 130 thousand copies in Japan.[46]

Another battle was being fought overseas, too. Atlus USA, a game publishing company in North America wanted to port *Demon's Souls* to North America out of respect for the graphics and pure challenge of the game. They started with a conservative sales estimate of seventy-five thousand units for their release in October 2009.[47] In reality, *Demon's Souls* ended up moving 280 thousand units by February

---

44   Nick Des Barres, "Japan Review Check: Demon's Souls," 1Up, January 28, 2019.

45   John Tanaka, "Tales of the World."

46   Japan Game Charts, "Japanese Total Sales from 11 November 2006 to 19 July 2009," Famitsu, August 9, 2009 distributed by The Internet Archive Wayback Machine.

47   Chris Remo, "Demon's Souls Sales Triple Atlus Expectations," Gamasutra, April 14, 2010.

2010.[48] Again, word of mouth among gamers in North America allowed this to happen.

Demon's Souls received raving reviews and sales numbers overseas. "[You] can remember the good ole days when games taught through the highly effective use of negative reinforcement," Sam Bishop of IGN said.[49]

After *Demon's Souls* was ported to the Americas and PAL (everywhere outside Japan and North America), sales skyrocketed. Within the span of just over a year, the game had sold over a million copies.[50]

Sony would come to regret their decision to not port *Demon's Souls* outside of Asia. Sony Japan's localization specialist, Yeonkyung Kim, stated as such in 2010 in an *Eurogamer* interview: "That was a mistake. It should have come out as a first-party title."[51]

Miyazaki's expectations had been upended. Some at Sony and FromSoftware were baffled. The game had seemed like a

---

48   "Demon's Souls Sells Triple What Atlus USA Expected," Silliconera, April 14, 2010.

49   Sam Bishop, "Demon's Souls Review," IGN, May 9, 2012.

50   "ゲーム制作未経験から世界的ヒット作「ダークソウル」を生んだ宮崎英高氏にインタビュー [From Inexperienced Game Developer to Worldwide Bestseller 'Dark Souls': An Interview with Hidetaka Miyazaki]," GigaZine, February 28, 2012.

51   Chris Remo, "Sony Regrets Not Publishing Demon's Souls in North America," Gamasutra, March 16, 2010.

complete programming and gameplay-side disaster up until release. How had it reached such numbers in sales?

The secret was its "classical" nature, wherein the development team tried to recreate the level of difficulty of "classic" games from their own childhoods. The game requires players to master complicated weapon and armor systems. Most games during the time were oversimplified with the intent of giving users easy-to-attain rewards in an attempt to get players hooked quickly and easily.

To elaborate, *Demon's Souls* has a cruel death penalty. If the player is killed, they are sent back to the beginning of the level with all enemies in that level re-appeared. The player respawns in "soul form," meaning they have less maximum health and have lost all of their unused "souls."[52] "Souls" in the game are equivalent to experience points that players can use to upgrade their stats. If the player is able to reach the location where they died, they will regain their lost souls. However, if they're killed in "soul form," they lose those souls permanently.

"The main concept behind the death system is trial and error," Miyazaki explained. "There are no other specific games that inspired this unique design."[53] He reiterates it was this desire to give a true sense of accomplishment to the player that drove the game design.

---

52 Sam Bishop, "Demon's Souls Review."

53 Keza MacDonald, "Tough Love: On Dark Souls' Difficulty," *Eurogamer*, December 7, 2019.

What may help us to understand the motivation for *why* and how this game came to fruition is to study Miyazaki's thoughts instead. Miyazaki's attitude toward the world is not one of hope or optimism, but rather realistic pessimism. "Light looks more beautiful in darkness," said Miyazaki during an interview in 2019.[54] "Personally, a world that is happy and bright is something that just doesn't feel realistic to me. It may sound like I have a trauma or something, but I believe that the world is generally a wasteland that is not kind to us."

His attitude is reflected in his games. Gore, death, and violence are ubiquitous, and players would be hard-pressed to find things of "true" beauty within these worlds. Whether or not this attitude is realistic or pessimistic or as violent and harsh as the ones portrayed in the *Dark Souls* series, or whether you stand up to its trials or not, are up to players.

Demon's Souls also had a unique style of asynchronous multiplayer.[55] Instead of a map on which players would fight against others online in real-time, in *Demon's Souls*, players could see actions of other players in the form of translucent "ghosts," not in real-time, in their own single-player games. Those other players' ghosts could also leave messages in the form of text on the floor. The purpose of this was to allow players to give hints to other players. Want to show a fellow *Demon's Souls* player the location of a hidden hallway

---

54   Esra Krabbe, "Elden Ring Is an Evolution of Dark Souls Says Creator – E3 2019," IGN, June 21, 2019.

55   Matt Kim, "Demon's Souls' Online Service Transformed Its Multiplayer Into a Literal Ghost Story," USG, November 27, 2017.

promising gold? You can do that. Want to trick somebody into a gruesome death? You can do that, too.

This asynchronous multiplayer was inspired directly by Miyazaki's transient encounter with the other drivers on the snowbank. He'd been both confused and grateful for the help of strangers, realizing that the relationship of all of the drivers there was fleeting and yet still feeling a sense of camaraderie within that helpless moment of losing control of one's car. He wanted to reflect that sense of helplessness and helpfulness in *Demon's Souls*.

Still, Miyazaki hoped that the "soul form" death system would encourage players to collaborate helpfully. It was this experience that motivated Miyazaki to create a system wherein players could help each other out without promise of reward.

With both the unique multiplayer-like gameplay mechanics and the difficulty, Miyazaki upended gaming norms of his era. Just like his career switch, he proved that he could subvert expectations by creating something that was thought to be impossible before.

After the success of *Demon's Souls*, *Dark Souls* followed in 2011 as a spiritual successor. Similar in both gameplay and mechanics, the game outsold *Demon's Souls* total sales in just one week of release. *Dark Souls'* slogan, again, promised one thing: "Prepare to die." And die the players did.[56]

---

56   Keza MacDonald, "The Mind Behind."

After *Dark Souls* came *Dark Souls II* (2014), *Dark Souls III* (2016), and *Dark Souls Remastered* (2018). All three have been lauded as masterpieces in their own right and exceptional sequels to the original promise of death and the challenge that comes along with it. The franchise, so far, has sold over twenty-five million copies worldwide.[57] And now, as From-Software's president, Miyazaki has more games in store that have many fans waiting for their release.

Miyazaki's cruel and innovative game development style reflects the challenges he faced entering the game development industry. From a childhood of poverty, he managed to get into a prestigious university, and he turned down the "one opportunity he had," as some would call it, to chase his dream. He didn't apply to a game development company straight out of college. Some could call that him setting himself up for a lifetime of failure.

Not Miyazaki. After being inspired by friends and his love of gaming, combined with the sheer boredom of his desk job, he made the leap of applying to other companies—and he just managed to find one that would take him.

Maybe some would call that luck. Or maybe it was the mindset that life can and will be cruel to you—unless you take that risky leap forward to that dream job you've always wanted.

---

57   "Press Release - New Action RPG 'Elden Ring' Announced," FromSoftware, accessed August 21, 2020.

CHAPTER 3

NETWORKS

---

*"Who would've thought back in the '80s
and '90s that literally everybody would be a
gamer. [Back then] it was a hobby [for us]...We
didn't actually think it was going to move this
fast. We thought eventually everybody would
be a gamer, because it's too fricking fun for
people to not be gamers. But we didn't know
it was gonna take over in two generations."*

—GORDON WALTON

When Gordon Walton told the United States Army that he
wanted to work on computers as his specialty in 1974, he
didn't realize he'd have to climb hundred-foot-tall poles in
Germany to work on signal wiring. "I was deathly afraid of
heights," he said in a college guest lecture at the University

of Texas at Austin.[58] "I wouldn't trade the first six months of the army for almost anything, but the other two and a half years, I could've done without."

As soon as he was finished with his service, his friend who was still in the army offered to take Walton to play games on military computers. His friend had access to the PLATO (Programmed Logic for Automated Teaching Operations) system: a multiplayer mainframe computer console intended to teach military recruits how to engage in combat that displayed everything in fluorescent green over a black background. Originally a computer-assisted instruction manual created in 1960, it ballooned to become supported on several thousand graphics terminals that were all connected over a mainframe network.

"And of course, what is everybody doing on there? They're playing games," Walton explained.[59] He had always been a tinkerer of electronics and programming and he figured that he might as well pass to look like he still served while "playing" on military-grade computer terminals. On them, he could play and create more single-player *and* multiplayer games, which he'd never had access to before. "I thought, 'How hard could that be?'...And it's a slippery slope [from there]," he described to me during our interview.

Walton knew he needed a university degree if he wanted to work in computing. So in 1978, Walton went to Texas A&M

---

58 *Gamedevthings*, "Warren Spector Lecture 11 - Gordon Walton," October 4, 2011, video, 2:44:21.

59 Ibid.

University in College Station, Texas, to earn a Bachelor of Science in computer science with a minor in electrical engineering. During this time, he also started to establish himself as an independent game author. At the time, microcomputers were not yet a "thing"—instead, at college, he typed all code into assembly language, and he'd typically have to wait overnight to see the results of their inputs.

When some of the first microcomputers started to come out in late 1977, he knew he had to get his hands on them. They were much faster and easier to program than mainframe computers. He had a decision to make, though: he could either buy a computer to practice programming, visit Europe to see his friends from the Army again, or he could buy a car for himself.

He went for the computer: a Commodore PET. He went on to establish himself as a game developer, publishing his work through Instant Software as an early game publisher, which was part of *Kilobaud* magazine including games like *Trek-X* (1977) and *Dungeon of Death* (1978). These games did not include color, so the display was limited to dungeon walls being depicted by single lines or, at best, tiles made to look like stone brick.[60]

Walton continued his journey through programming, then management until he decided to cofound Applied Computing (later called Digital Illusions) with his friend, Don Gilman in 1985. Though he'd be in the position of president, he

---

60   Chester Bolingbroke, "Game 86: Dungeon of Death (1979)," *CRPG Addict* (blog), February 7, 2013.

wanted to focus on the game development itself instead of the managing of people doing the development or selling of the products. At Applied Computing, he worked on several Macintosh games: *Orbiter* (1986), *Sub Battle Simulator* (1987), *Reader Rabbit* (1987), *NFL Challenge* (1987), and *PT-109* (1988), to name a few popular hits.

These games were then starting to take advantage of graphics.[61] Of course, compared to the graphics of today, they're not much to brag about; but for back then, they were revolutionary. *Sub Battle Simulator's* opening title screen included a rather detailed drawing of a sub emerging from the ocean with enough color samples of blue and white to re-create ocean surf. The game even included a user interface (UI) to make the player feel as though they were really controlling a submarine.

Coming from a time where just a few years ago, "Most people didn't even know [about gaming]...If they did, they thought it was the Pac-Man machine at the pizza parlor," as he described it. A drastic change in production quality occurred throughout the late '80s. Instead of green glowing lines of text on military machines, games were beginning to imitate reality. And instead of bringing your children to the barbershop for them to play *Pong* while they wait for their haircut, it was becoming possible to meet people from around the world and communicate with them over the interface of a video game.

---

61   "Sub Battle Simulator Download (1987 Simulation Game)," Old-Games, accessed September 21, 2020.

After having worked in a more hands-on setting, Walton found he needed to return to management of game development if he wanted to make an impact. In any industry, it's uncommon to stay doing what you love for long if you want to leave your mark. You have to accept that more often than not, you're going to get promoted and you won't be able to continue doing what you love—you'll have to manage it instead. When I asked which Walton would rather be doing, he exclaimed, "Of course I'd rather be working on game development!"

Walton departed Digital Illusions in 1989 to bounce back and forth between four management positions in four years—as he said during our interview, "I could never hold a steady job"—until he reached Kesmai Corporation in 1995. There, he worked as senior vice president and the general studio manager for four years. Walton worked on massively multiplayer online ("MMO") games such as *Air Warrior II-III* (1997, 1997) and *Legends of Kesmai* (1996). This was around the time he first began to touch upon a new genre: Massively Multiplayer Online (MMO) games.

His work at Kesmai marked a new chapter of his life: working on massively multiplayer online role-playing games ("MMORPG") instead of single-player. The development of multiplayer games is far different from those of single-player, simply because they require such an intimate relationship with the player fanbase. Because multiplayer games are generally subscription-based, and the nature of multiplayer enables and encourages players to find bugs in-game, the developers must take an active role in fixing those bugs. This is why many multiplayer games typically release as "alpha/

beta" pre-versions, and not a "one-and-done" release, which is common for single-player (though not so much today).

Still, it wasn't until Walton moved to working at Origin Systems in March of 1999 that he truly began to find what he enjoyed doing. At Origin, Walton says, he was able to make the "biggest difference" in something he truly cared about. A major part of that came from his contributions to the *Ultima Online* (1997) online service as the vice president and executive producer.

The game is an MMORPG set in a fantasy universe called "Britannia." The game features a complex player versus player (PVP) combat system that it became well-known for. The online service, in order to give you context, is a service that is still active to this day, over twenty years later.

---

62   *Gamedevthings*, "Warren Spector Lecture 11."

This is all in spite of then-predictions that saw Internet gaming as an incredible gamble. A *CNNMoney* article from August 1999 declared: "Sony, Sega, Microsoft, and Electronic Arts are betting that games played over the Internet will be the biggest thing since Monopoly." That same article goes on to describe how people were selling real-life money, sometimes in the hundreds of dollars, for in-game items in *Ultima Online*.[63] At the time, such a thing was completely absurd. Spending $1,000 on an exclusive castle with dragons on the property? In a *video game*? It was laughable.

Still, *Ultima Online* quickly became one of the most commercially successful internet-based multiplayer games ever. It sold sixty-five thousand units in less than two months, with so much demand that pre-orders were delayed and stores ran out of stock of copies.[64] Consider that the retail price for the game was $40 to $70, plus a $10/month subscription fee. It was a trailblazer in a field that no other electronic giant had ventured into.

"It was a great game with a great community," Walton responded when I asked just what working on the project was like. "Every workday was chaotic, since there were a lot of operational, service, code problems. But I knew I was making a difference to the medium, since I had the right skills at the time." Because of his previous work on multiplayer

63   Marc Gunther, "The Newest Addiction Sony, Sega, Microsoft, and Electronic Arts Are Betting That Games Played over the Internet Will Be the Biggest Thing since Monopoly," *CNN Money*, August 2, 1999.

64   PC Gamer Online, "UbiSoft's Tonic Trouble," Imagine Publishing, November 10, 1997, distributed by The Internet Archive Wayback Machine.

games at Kesmai, as well as his general knowledge of game programming, his talents shined.

So when Maxis, the development company of *The Sims* (2000), asked Walton to manage the development of a new, MMO *Sims* game, his initial reaction was to refuse the offer. He had a great job working on *Ultima*, after all. It was only after much convincing about how Walton could contribute to the future of the medium that he acquiesced. "[Maxis] literally came and dragged me out of something I was having a great time doing because it was so important to the business."

Maxis had just released *The Sims* to critical acclaim, and they now wanted to develop an online version of the game to hop onto the bandwagon that *Ultima Online* was riding. But they knew it was the early years of online MMO game development, and they wanted to ensure their game wouldn't fail. "Ninety percent of all [MMO] games failed miserably," Walton recalled. But Maxis had a vision. They'd seen what Walton had been able to pull off for *Ultima Online* at Origin, and they wanted him to repeat that—for Maxis and Electronic Arts, this time.

Unfortunately, development was difficult from the beginning. "It was already a clusterfuck from the first quarter," Walton explained. There was the constant chaos of building a stable multiplayer network that could support the many thousands EA was expecting. There was the added pressure of EA, their publisher, expecting the game to be ready to ship by a certain date, whether or not the game was ready. "It was like rowing upstream the whole way."

Constant bugs, tension in the team, and other issues led to a complete failure of *The Sims Online* upon release.[65] The economy was broken, using money wasn't even all that rewarding, and players couldn't create custom content, called "mods," for *The Sims Online*, like they'd done for *The Sims*. Add to that the fact that the idea of setting up an MMO for casual players in a time when people were still throwing out their dial-up modems to transition to cable/DSL Internet, and it was a clear financial failure in EA's eyes. They cancelled the production of the game and turned Maxis, their developer, to work on non-MMO sequels of *The Sims*.

After having worked on *The Sims Online*, Walton gave a talk at the Game Developers' Conference in 2003 entitled, "Ten Great Reasons You Don't want to Make a Massively Multiplayer Game." In it, some reasons he listed included "7. Getting a Credit Card from a Customer is *Hard*" and "4. The Internet Sucks as a Commercial Delivery Platform."[66] This garnered him fame within the game development community.

In spite of the failure of *The Sims Online*, Walton wasn't discouraged from the medium. "Most game makers are not really into the money," Walton elaborated. "I'm looking for impact, perhaps more than anything else." Walton continued similar positions through the later 2000s and '10s, like Sony Online, BioWare, and Playdom, garnering thanks and credits

65   Lisa Nguyen, "15 Shocking Things You Didn't Know about the Miserable Sims Online," The Gamer, September 24, 2017.

66   Dave Kosak, "Ten Reasons You Don't Want to Run a Massively Multiplayer Online Game," GameSpy, March 7, 2003, distributed by The Internet Archive Wayback Machine.

on games like *Star Wars: Galaxies* (2004) and *Star Wars: The Old Republic* (2011).

Since then, Walton has also moved on to his own endeavors. When he moved back to Austin, Texas, in 2005, he started working at Austin Community College and the University of Texas at Austin as an advisory board member to their gaming programs. He cofounded his own company, ArtCraft Entertainment, which has been working on a crowdfunded MMO game called *Crowfall* since 2013. There, he works as president and executive producer of the company to this day. He manages the finances, production, development, and overall studio.

Crowfall is impressive in that it crowdfunded $1.77 million of its $800,000 goal. Crowdfunding is what it sounds like: a group of people online contribute funds to the development of a project (a game, in this case). Game developers often choose the route of crowdfunding either when they don't want to deal with the expectations of a publisher, or when they can't find a publisher.

If the contribution goals are met, the project will be developed (key word: developed, not *successful;* some online crowdfunding sites provide protections to contributors if the project is a fraud). Crowdfunding was also used to create this very book!

Walton admits that crowdfunding is not an equal playing field. "We cheated, of course," he exclaimed. "[Crowdfunding] is a game and you need an unfair advantage to make it happen. My partner and I both had access to the press. That separates us from 99 percent of the people who are doing Kickstarters (a popular crowdfunding site)."

Crowdfunding has become a more and more popular source of raising necessary funds to make a game since the 2010s. Well-known games like *Pillars of Eternity* (2015) and *Shovel Knight* (2014) were crowdfunded. For *Crowfall*, Walton felt crowdfunding was the best choice.

When it comes down to it, Walton is most interested in leaving an impact on the industry. "You need to find something about every project that excites you," he said. His goal in life was to always strive for purpose and making the most use out of himself that he could. Most of the time, that was as an executive producer or director managing the project. It's important to consider the implications of these decisions before making them.

CHAPTER 4

TO FAIL TO SUCCEED

———

"The minute you don't want to call someone is the minute you have to call them...In business, I was very shy, I didn't like confrontation, but I had to really learn that 'now' is what matters."[67]

—FEARGUS URQUHART

Overseeing a video game development company is difficult. As we've seen with Cage, Miyazaki, and Walton, adapting to the constant shifts and updates to software and skillsets is challenging. It is crucial to adapt a mindset of humility and gratitude in order to stay a CEO of a game company for longer than a couple years. Perhaps nobody better exemplifies that than Feargus Urquhart.

———

67   *Digital Dragons*, "DD 2016 - Feargus Urquhart: 25 Years Down, 25 Years to Go: A Life Creating Games," June 1 2016, video, 48:13.

Urquhart is one of those successful CEO game developers—though you wouldn't know it from talking to him. He's gathered a significant amount of fame as the father of the *Fallout* series and as the president of Obsidian Entertainment, and developer of highly successful games such as *Star Wars: Knights of the Old Republic* (2003), *Fallout* (1997) and, recently, *The Outer Worlds* (2020).

Urquhart started out as an engineering major at University of California (UC) Riverside in 1988, sticking around until 1990. He then transferred to UC San Diego (UCSD) to pursue a bioengineering major from 1990 to 1994. He started to work as a playtester over the summers of 1991 through 1993 for video games developed at Interplay Productions, a local game publisher and development company in Los Angeles, California. In spite of the many years he spent in secondary education, he never completed either degree—he left in the last couple of months, when the only classes he had left were three more electives, to pursue a permanent position at Interplay.

Because engineering majors are notorious for their post-graduate job stability and high income, I was expecting a significant fall-out story from Urquhart when I asked him about it.

"My dad was...unhappy because the playtesting job was a summer job, and I really only had three classes to go," Urquhart explained.

In some families, it's an unfortunate reality that parents highly disapprove of their child's pursuits of pursuing video game development that persists to this day. But Urquhart was one of those lucky few who didn't receive much resistance at all.

During his time at Interplay, Urquhart playtested games like *RPM Racing* (1991), *Star Trek 25th Anniversary* (1992), and *Mario Teaches Typing* (1992) for the SNES and personal computer system, and reported bugs when he found them.[68] (Not the worst summer job, if you ask me.) The gig landed him a further role at Interplay as a Producer in 1993—hence the dropping out of college in 1994, when Interplay had just created a dedicated "RPG Division." This role consisted more of managing relationships with both internal and external developers, such as BioWare and Blizzard Entertainment. As producer, he managed projects like *Baldur's Gate* (1998) and *The Lost Vikings II* (1997) instead of the previous playtesting.

Funnily enough, he had a sit-down conversation with his father. When his father asked Urquhart how much he made and he responded, his father just said, "Well, you made a good choice because you're obviously enjoying what you're doing...and money-wise, [it's the same as engineering]."

As time went on, Urquhart danced with both the game development-side and the managerial-side until he was promoted to director of the RPG division in 1996 and, later, president. Here, he became responsible over every part of the game product: development, production, and marketing were all fair game.

---

68   "Mario Teaches Typing," Interplay Entertainment Corp., 1992, accessed August 30, 2020, distributed by Archive.org.

"We were still...learning the industry," Urquhart described of his work at that time. On one particular game, *Shattered Steel* (1996), made by BioWare, Urquhart elaborated on his more hands-on roles, even as a director of the RPG division. "Their development team was super small back then, like ten people...I'd write all the dialogue for the cutscenes. I'm not an artist by any stretch of the means, but I sketched out some stick figures for the layout of the cutscenes."

One of the games Black Isle Studios worked on was *Fallout: A Post Nuclear Role Playing Game*, released in 1997. It was a groundbreaking, open-world post-apocalyptic game inspired by the post-war culture of the 1950s in the United States. Urquhart worked hands-on on a number of *Fallout*'s design innovations.

Fallout had a spiritual predecessor—*Wasteland* (1988)—developed by Interplay, which used more tabletop role-playing mechanics. Still, the plot was the same: survive the post-apocalyptic wasteland. *Wasteland* has also garnered favorable reviews, ranked number eleven in *Computer Gaming World*'s 1990 survey of magazine readers' "All-Time Favorite" games.[69] It made sense Interplay would develop similar games once they had discovered a market to tap into.

The reason for *Fallout*'s all-out success was its unique game mechanics and style. Most games at the time were fantasy- or space-based, where players had to simply defeat monsters in

---

69   "The Top Ten Games," Computer Gaming World Museum, Computer Gaming World 67, no. 67 (1990): 44, distributed by The Internet Archive Wayback Machine.

battle. The RPG genre was experiencing a notorious slump: "If October [1997]'s list is any indication, RPGs are back," wrote one commenter.[70] *Fallout* took upon itself to invent a new story and create fresh yet complex dialogue, combat, and worlds that both critics and players loved. *Fallout* moved over fifty thousand units by the end of 1997 and went on to sell over six hundred thousand copies.[71]

Due to the commercial success of *Fallout*, Interplay decided to follow it up with a sequel: *Fallout 2* (1998). At this time, the RPG Division was renamed to Black Isle Studios with the launch of *Fallout 2*. Urquhart worked as lead designer, acting more as overhead this time. "I designed some of the areas, I managed the designers, I...guided the story," Urquhart described of his roles. During the middle of development, he promoted another designer on the team to work as the co-lead designer, who worked on the nuts and bolts of the systems, while Urquhart and the designer both focused on how the story and flow of the areas came together.

FUN FACTS:
Games He's Worked On: *Fallout* (1997), *Star Wars: Knights of the Old Republic* (2003), *The Outer Worlds* (2020)
Companies Worked: Interplay, Obsidian Entertainment
Game he would like to create with infinite resources: An urban fantasy RPG like CD Projekt Red's *Cyberpunk*

---

70   GamerX, "October's Best-Sellers," CNet Game Center, November 26, 1997, distributed by The Internet Archive Wayback Machine.

71   RPGCodex, "RPG Codex Report: A Codexian Visit to inXile Entertainment," InXile Entertainment, April 13, 2017.

2077 (2020), but with elves and dwarves. He loves games that look like you're in the modern world but has been alternated as well. However, he doesn't want infinite resources. Instead, would like somebody to give him a fair amount of resources and time to create something. When you have infinite resources and infinite time, you have no reason to ever make something. There needs to be pressure.

Favorite Games: RPGs like *Dungeons & Dragons* (1974), *Twilight 2000* (1984), *Cyberpunk 2077* (2020)[72]

Urquhart refers a concept known as the "Scott Everts Paradox," named after a designer of *Fallout* and *Fallout 2*. Everts was a level designer, and the only level layout designer. He manually designed every single tile in *Fallout*, and placed regular tiles, trap tiles, and items on the floor by hand.

But for *Fallout 2*, when Urquhart transferred another level designer to work with Everts, a problem arose. When he watched the new designer working with the tools, he couldn't help but wonder why the designer didn't just copy and paste the structures in the game and then modify it. Instead, the new designer manually placed each tile. Why didn't the designer just use copy and paste? Surely, Everts used it. However, the answer was simple: the level editor had no copy and paste function.

"There's no copy and paste function?" Urquhart responded with horror.[73] He went to confront Scott Everts, who,

---

72   *IGN*, "Legendary RPG Developer Feargus Urquhart - IGN Unfiltered 15," January 31, 2017, video, 1:07:03.

73   *Digital Dragons*, "DD 2016 - Feargus Urquhart."

when asked about the issue, meekly answered that he knew about the problem. Why? "He didn't want to bother the programmers."

Urquhart wasn't happy, to say the least. He had a million other responsibilities to deal with, and for some godforsaken reason, there was no copy and paste function in a game where giant chunks of the map were the exact same tile.

So, Urquhart took Everts to visit the programmers to ask them how long it would take to develop this function. The answer was three days. When Urquhart asked Everts how much time this would've saved him, he answered, "I don't wanna talk about it."

And herein lies one of Urquhart's favorite lessons: never make assumptions. He's found it's vital in business to ask the stupid questions we're all embarrassed to ask.

Fallout 2 still went on to be a commercially successful game, selling 120 thousand copies within two years.[74] It received rave reviews for its gameplay and storyline, but was criticized for its frequent bugs.[75]

During this time, in spite of the great work being done at Black Isle Studios, their "parent" division, Interplay, was

---

74   "Desslock's Ramblings — RPG Sales Figures," Desslock's RPG News Archives, GameSpot, May 11, 2000, distributed by The Internet Archive Wayback Machine.

75   Daniel Morris, "Fallout 2," GamePro, January 1, 2000, distributed by The Internet Archive Wayback Machine.

failing financially. In 1998, it ran into financial problems while attempting to go public, with added lack of financial returns on its sports division games and lack of console titles, and it was bought out by Titus Interactive, a Paris-based game company over the course of 1999 to 2001.[76]

By 2003, Urquhart had grown frustrated. He felt that no matter how good of a job his studio did in producing a game, their next game had to be done for less money, and faster. While their games were successful, their RPG division was not prioritized. For example, at one point, it took six months to get new computers approved—previous requests for new computers were unapproved multiple times.

He had two options. He could become a game developer for another local company in the area where he lived in Orange County, California, like Blizzard Entertainment (which he hoped would take him), or found his own independent game development studio.

He decided to leave Black Isle Studio to establish his own game company in 2003. It would be called Obsidian Entertainment. When I asked why he did so, he initially joked, "Because I didn't know better," but he followed up: "I just felt...we had something to offer." He had worked on role-playing games, which he loved, and he and his coworkers were already well-known. They didn't have to hack-and-claw their way up the game developer food chain—they already had a huge base of support who would buy their games. Plus, they

76   P.J. Huffstutter, "Investment in Interplay," *Los Angeles Times*, May 13, 1999.

felt that if they didn't do it then, they wouldn't have done it. They would've played it safe and worked for other companies because among him and his coworkers, many were going to or already had children (Urquhart's wife was pregnant at the time) and many had mortgages.

Since its founding, Obsidian has produced many successful, well-known games: *Star Wars: Knights of the Old Republic* (2003), *Fallout: New Vegas* (2010), *South Park: The Stick of Truth* (2014), and *Pillars of Eternity* (2015), to name a few.

Perhaps one of the greatest strengths Urquhart has is a healthy mindset toward his career. One mindset he holds near is "Kaizen," a Japanese concept that came from the Toyota company referring to the idea of constant improvement of oneself so that one may better themselves and the company they work for. "Today is a new day...[yesterday] is [old news]," Urquhart preached at his talk to fellow game developers at a Digital Dragons conference in 2016 entitled "25 years down, 25 years left to go."[77]

If an entry-level programmer makes a mistake, a playtester will catch it. However, if Urquhart makes a mistake, it might cost several million dollars. "It's hard to wake up the next morning and go, 'Okay, now I gotta make games again.' Games are supposed to be fun. This doesn't seem fun anymore..."[78] He must wake up the next morning and remind himself that "today is a new day." That doesn't mean ignoring the problem—it simply means having a rational attitude

---

77   *Digital Dragons*, "DD 2016 - Feargus Urquhart."

78   Ibid.

toward it, because getting emotional over failure doesn't help when you're a CEO and you're signing off on the same big business decisions the next day.

His final principle, and perhaps his most important, is that we are game developers because we love games. "There's been times where...I was getting in my car telling my wife I'm going to drive in and resign," he admitted. But he reminds himself of why he does this, and how he got into this role in the first place. It's because he loves games. And it's important to exercise that love, too. "I will not play a game for six weeks, and then I'll go, 'How the heck did I not play a game for six weeks?!'"[79]

We must understand that this is a labor of love, not of convenience or money. Being a CEO of a company is often a drain on a person, and often requires sacrifice, whether that means a university degree (in the short term), relationships, or short-term financial gain. It requires risk, as Urquhart demonstrated by leaving Interplay to create his own company. The fact that his coworkers from Black Isle followed him to Obsidian also shows Urquhart's responsibility and his personable nature.

Many factors make a company successful. A gaming company, even more so. Urquhart demonstrates these qualities through his humility and ambition, and his willingness to accept failure. Anyone who wants to last in a powerful position at a gaming company must adopt this mindset.

---

79 Ibid.

CHAPTER 5

THE GAMER HEARD ROUND THE WORLD

———

"Above all, video games are meant to be just one thing: fun. Fun for everyone." [80]

—SATORU IWATA

"On my business card, I am a corporate president. In my mind, I am a game developer. But in my heart, I am a gamer."[81] These are the famous words spoken by Satoru Iwata, former CEO of Nintendo of Japan, at his speech chronicling his journey into game development at the annual Game Developers Conference in 2005, before his dive into fame. These words left a mark on a generation of gamers and game developers—but why? What was so significant about these words, and why did they have such an influence back in 2005?

———

80 Justin Davis, "11 Memorable Satoru Iwata Quotes," IGN Entertainment, July 13, 2015.

81 *GDC*, "Satoru Iwata - Heart of a Gamer," July 14, 2015, video, 1:00:22.

Iwata is one of the most famous and respected game developers of our time because despite his accomplishments, he was always humble and personable. In spite of health complications and business challenges, he faced them with respect and joyfulness. Let us take a look through his work, and how he became the president of one of the most successful gaming companies in the world.

Satoru Iwata wasn't initially a poor or unsuccessful man by any means. Born in Sapporo, Japan, in 1959, the prefecture of which his father was a local elected official, Iwata was a natural-born leader who followed in his father's footsteps by becoming class president, student council president, and club president in school.[82]

Ever since he was young, Iwata was fascinated by game development. By the time he was in high school in 1975, he was one of the first in his class to purchase an HP-65 calculator, the first card-programmable handheld calculator going for $795 MSRP in 1974, or equivalent to over $4,000 in 2020.[83]

The first game he ever programmed was a baseball game. "I don't think anyone can say it has bad graphics, because it [had] no graphics," Iwata joked. "When I saw my friends playing that game and having fun, it made me feel proud. For me, this was a source of energy and passion."[84] That

82   Osamu Inoue, *Nintendo Magic: Winning the Videogame Wars* (New York: Vertical, Inc., 2010), 56.

83   "HP-65 Programmable Pocket Calculator, 1974," Hewlett-Packard Development Company, L.P., accessed August 30, 2020.

84   *GDC*, "Satoru Iwata - Heart of a Gamer."

moment of youthful helped him to realize a passion for game development.

In 1978, Iwata entered the prestigious Tokyo Institute of Technology to study computer programming. He admitted he would've studied video game programming specifically if he could've, it just wasn't offered at the time.[85]

While his friends went home to study, Iwata often headed to the first major retail store in the city of Tokyo that had just started to sell dedicated personal computers. "That was my hangout," Iwata recalled.[86] He made friends there, and they all thought about how to create, program, and design games for these computers. Soon after, they rented an apartment in Tokyo to start programming games.

All of this was happening while Iwata was a university student. He studied by day and programmed with friends by night.

That group of friends in the apartment in Tokyo would eventually become HAL Laboratory, a game development company, and as Iwata continued with his studies, he started working there as an assistant. Yash Terakura, an employee of HAL Laboratory who mentored Iwata, recalled, "Iwata was stopping by my office almost every day after school...He helped me make test programs...so that he could obtain news about our new products, as well as technical information not

85 Ibid.
86 Ibid.

available to the public."[87] Through showing such diligence, Iwata eventually took up a part-time position at HAL in 1980 during his sophomore year of college to work as a programmer for his devotion to the company.

While at HAL, he worked on multiple games that were "pretty much rip offs of Namco's *Rally-X* (1980) and *Galaxian* (1982) games," according to him in a 1999 interview for *Used Games Magazine*.[88] However, their work was respectable, considering the fact that they built the graphics capability themselves, on a then-famous hardware peripheral they created called the "PCG" (perhaps standing for "Peripheral Component Graphics").[89]

This endeavor was impressive enough that Namco themselves decided to work with HAL as an external developer for the first time in Namco's history. Iwata was on track to finish up his studies at Tokyo Institute of Technology in 1982 and join HAL Laboratory as an official employee soon thereafter.

FUN FACTS:
Games He's Worked On: *Kirby's Dream Land* (1992), *Earthbound/Mother II* (1994), *Super Mario Galaxy* (2007)
Companies Worked: HAL Laboratory, Nintendo

---

87   John Andersen, "A Former Mentor Recalls the Early Career of Satoru Iwata," Gamasutra, October 9, 2015.

88   "Satoru Iwata - 1999 Developer Interview," Used Games Magazine, distributed by Shmuplations, accessed August 30, 2020.

89   Ibid.

Things were looking good, at least professionally, though he remarked that at his graduation, he was the graduate joining the smallest company out of all his classmates.[90] His father was highly disapproving of Iwata's work. He had just been elected mayor of Muroran, a city of lower Hokkaido, and had expected nobler pursuits from his son.[91] He refused to speak to Iwata for six months after finding out his career choice.[92]

"[He] must have thought I was joining a religious cult," Iwata admitted, though he laughed about it after the fact.[93] Working on video games in the early '80s was one thing; joining a tiny company that no one had ever heard of after attending the Tokyo Institute of Technology was like a slap in the face, especially in Japan, where the tradition of "Oyakoukou," or filial piety, is well practiced.

Still, despite these familial challenges, things were generally looking up for Iwata, business- and career-wise. He did the programming, marketing, and design for games and even ordered takeout for him and his coworkers. And a new rumor was circulating that Nintendo was planning to release the Famicom (the adored NES in Americas), and, with it, a much higher resolution graphics capability.[94] And HAL had ideas for graphics.

90   GDC, "Satoru Iwata - Heart of a Gamer."

91   Inoue, Nintendo Magic, 58.

92   "Profile: Satoru Iwata," IGN Entertainment, last updated June 17, 2012.

93   Ibid; GDC, "Satoru Iwata - Heart of a Gamer."

94   Ibid.

HAL did everything they could to try and get in contact with Nintendo to convince them to publish one of their games. Their plans succeeded, but with limitations. Nintendo did hire them, but Nintendo wanted HAL to repair one of their failed projects, *Pin Ball* (1983), first.

Because *Pin Ball* was the first time HAL got to work on creating a game for the NES, they had to learn how the hardware worked with the software of the game. By taking advantage of Iwata's deep understanding of the relationship between hardware and software, they learned how to portray creatures, items, and abstract concepts as art that the player could easily understand.[95] Their work was impressive enough for Nintendo to consider them as a long-term business partner.

Game development in the early 1980s was also vastly different from what it is now. "The concept of 'director' didn't really exist yet," Iwata explains. "The programmer himself would make a lot of decisions about the content, making guesses about how players would react to such-and-such idea. Then we'd show what we made to Nintendo, who would give their advice, and we would go back and revise it."[96]

Both Iwata and HAL were proving themselves exceptional in game development. For example, Nintendo had been struggling to find a developer that would agree to program eighteen golf courses into extremely limited memory for a game on the NES. When Nintendo came around to ask HAL, Iwata leapt to the task. "I'll do it!" After all, one of Iwata's

---

95   Ibid.

96   "Satoru Iwata - 1999 Developer Interview," Used Games Magazine.

main philosophies in game development is the idea that the moment a programmer says, "I can't do that," the idea dies.[97] The programmer is always the gatekeeper to the creation of any game's design. That game would eventually become *Open Tournament Golf* (1987), and it would be one of the few Iwata worked on from start to finish, mostly by himself.

However, not everything they did was so lucky. In the early 1990s, HAL Laboratory created a vastly different game from what they had been working on before: *Metal Slader Glory* (1991). It was one of the most expensive Famicom games of its time, releasing for an extraordinary 8900 yen (or $89, equivalent to $164 in modern currency).[98*] The game advertised itself as having an "astonishing 8Mb cart size," and included graphics of characters venturing through space with robots and mechs.[99]

Unfortunately, the sales could simply not break even with merely the costs of marketing the game.[100] "Very few copies were produced and put in circulation. For that fact alone, I can't really praise it," Iwata commented.[101] The game was a severe financial failure, and the cost of its advertising, among

97   Ibid.

98   ˙ Most NES games at this time went for $49.99 (US), and sometimes as low as $29.99, though those were usually reserved for third-party games. Some games went for up to $59.99, but never $89.99.

99   Ibid.

100 Brian Crimmins, "Why Does HAL Laboratory Only Make Nintendo Games?," *Vice News*, November 21, 2017.

101 "Satoru Iwata - 1999 Developer Interview," Used Games Magazine.

other financial missteps, had led HAL Laboratory to the verge of bankruptcy by 1992.[102]

By this point, morale at HAL Laboratory had tanked. They had previously made great games for Nintendo, like *Pin Ball* and *Open Tournament Golf*—why couldn't they keep up their success? Would this tight-knit, small company collapse after all?

As HAL was on the verge of bankruptcy Iwata turned to his coworkers at HAL and declared, "Okay, from here on out, every game we create is going to sell a million copies!"[103] It would've been laughable had they not built up such a strong relationship with Nintendo. Hearing about HAL's crisis, Nintendo showed interest in supporting HAL Laboratory through any such financial disaster. But the support was conditional. Though Iwata has never publicly admitted what these conditions exactly were, he soon accepted the position as HAL's president in 1993—which many suspect was one of the prerequisites for Nintendo's continued support.[104]

To combat the bankruptcy, HAL started work on the game with their first IP: *Kirby's Dream Land* (1992).[105*] This time, Nintendo would publish the game for them, instead of doing

---

102   Martin Robinson, "Satoru Iwata: A Gentle Revolutionary," *Eurogamer*, July 14, 2015.

103   "Satoru Iwata - 1999 Developer Interview," Used Games Magazine.

104   Ibid.

105   * Notes: "IP", or *Intellectual Property*, came about as a way for developers to legally protect their own ideas, such as characters and story. It's the same legal protection given to books and films.

that work in-house. HAL took pitches from many of Nintendo's designers, and they liked Masahiro Sakurai's idea of "Twinkle Popo," a bouncy, cute character that literally sucks up enemies to absorb their powers. "Twinkle Popo" would later become "Kirby." It was intended to be a game that would be fun for anybody to play. This game would go on to be a great commercial success and act as HAL's mascot as a company. To date, the game has sold over five million copies, and Kirby's character continues to be used as one of Nintendo's main mascots.[106]

After saving HAL Laboratory, during a game expo, the president of Nintendo at the time, Hiroshi Yamauchi, the same person who had mentored Shigeru Miyamoto, mentioned "HAL Laboratory" in his speech thirteen times. The tone was rather optimistic for business: he stated how "he was looking forward to seeing how [HAL] turned out." Iwata mentions that at the time, he was "embarrassed to have the matter of our bankruptcy discussed in a public space like that, but now that I look back on it, I believe that he was really cheering us on."[107]

Iwata continued to demonstrate his leadership and perseverance while working as HAL's president. As it was, he often took it upon himself to study books on management so that he could work as the company president better.[108]

---

106 Osamu Inoue, "Iwata and Miyamoto: Business Ascetics - an Excerpt from Nintendo Magic," Gamasutra, May 14, 2010.

107 "Satoru Iwata - 1999 Developer Interview," Used Games Magazine.

108 Toshi Nakamura, "Smash Bros. Creator Remembers Satoru Iwata," Kotaku, July 22, 2015.

One example of this was during the development of *Mother 2* (1994) (*Earthbound* as it is commonly known in the Americas), a weird, wacky cult classic. HAL was asked by Nintendo for help because the original software developer, Ape, was falling far behind schedule.[109] They had worked on the game for over four years and they were completely stuck in development.

To ensure *Mother 2* succeeded, Iwata took the initiative to get into the nitty-gritty of programming himself to help the programmers at HAL and Ape. HAL employees were surprised that their now-company president was doing such a thing; but, after all, Iwata's main reason for getting into game development in the first place was his love for programming. Doing that, he managed to fix the programming bugs that Ape had worked on for years, in the span of six months.[110]

The success of *Mother 2* changed everyone's attitude at HAL—as well as Nintendo's view of Iwata. He continued to persevere in similar efforts. For example, he helped out GameFreak, a developer working with Nintendo, by reading the entire source code for *Pokémon Red* and *Pokémon Green* (1996) on the Game Boy console and translating the code into a battle system for *Pokémon Stadium* (1999) for the Nintendo 64.[111] "Is that guy a programmer? Or is he the president?" Shigeki Morimoto, one of Iwata's colleagues, remarked.[112]

109 "Satoru Iwata - 1999 Developer Interview," Used Games Magazine.

110 *GDC*, "Satoru Iwata - Heart of a Gamer."

111 Martin Robinson, "Satoru Iwata: A Gentle Revolutionary."

112 Iwata Asks, "Just Being President Was a Waste!," Nintendo, accessed August 30, 2020.

Following these efforts, it didn't come as much of a surprise that Yamauchi asked Iwata to succeed him as Nintendo's president in 2002. Iwata had already been working at Nintendo as its head of the corporate planning division since 2000. "I knew this would require committing much more time, and assuming much more responsibility," Iwata said. "Fortunately, game developers are familiar with such things."[113] He would succeed as the first Nintendo president unrelated to the Yamauchi family by blood or marriage since its founding in 1889.[114]

Iwata saw two things as problems with the current state of the game industry: the rise of improving graphics to the point of realism as much as possible in gaming. The first problem was simply a matter of money: graphics cards for the hardware cost a lot of money for the consumer. "Games are stuck," Iwata told *Mainichi*, a Japanese Newspaper company, in 2004. "We're creating too advanced of graphics in games, and it's not working anymore."[115]

The second problem, though, concerned the rise of game developers and publishing companies being out of touch with their audiences. Gaming companies were releasing games that were either too difficult or simply unappealing

---

113 GDC, "Satoru Iwata - Heart of a Gamer."

114 Liam Stack, "Satoru Iwata, Nintendo Chief Executive, Dies at 55," *The New York Times*, July 13, 2015.

115 "キーマンインタビュー→任天堂社長岩田聡さん：新ハードでびっくりさせる [Key Interview with Nintendo President Satoru Iwata: Surprise Them with New Hardware]," Mainichi Interactive, accessed August 30, 2020, distributed by The Internet Archive Wayback Machine.

to mainstream audiences. Nintendo was no exception: consider the term "Nintendo hard," used as a way to refer to the difficulty of many earlier Nintendo games in the '80s and '90s, like *Contra* (1988) and *Ninja Gaiden* (1988).

The reason for this phenomenon? As Iwata put it, this was because everyone involved in the production of games would play the games all the time for bug-testing purposes and hence lose all sense of how difficult the game was for a beginner.[116]

Iwata wanted to follow Itoi's practice during the production of *Mother 2*—Itoi wrote that a part of the game's target audience were "children, adults, and [your] older sister" who should be able to play the game.[117] However, gaming still stayed away from these target audiences in the early 2000s, whom Iwata thought Nintendo could capitalize on.

These realizations that Iwata had were what made his speech in 2005 at the United States Game Developers' Conference so influential. A video game development company president, let alone a Japanese one, being *personable* and *open* in a conference event? Unheard of. The fact that he was speaking in English with a noticeable Japanese accent for an hour was also highly unusual. Yet his speech drew excitement for the future of Nintendo and gaming. He detailed his own life experiences in detail, proving his devotion to his position not just as a business executive, but as a gamer and game

116   Mike Williams, "Teens React to Mega Man: What We've Forgotten about 'Nintendo Hard' Games," USGamer, December 15, 2014.

117   "[Key Interview with Nintendo President]," Mainichi Interactive.

developer. It was a promise that Nintendo would do better and listen to its consumers.

Both the DS and the Wii went on to rank among the top six best-selling gaming platforms of all time, and with good reason: Iwata had led Nintendo by capitalizing on several different markets that other gaming companies had refused to do, like the young, the old, and women.[118]

It's important to realize that Iwata's decisions were met with widespread criticism. "Iwata says he has the heart of a gamer... What poor bastard did he carve it from?" Greg Costikyan, a long-time gaming industry veteran, criticized at the 2005 Game Developers' Conference, in reaction to Nintendo's keynote presentation about their new company mission.[119]

Iwata also made strange requests to production teams, like: "make it so [the DS] could survive being dropped from 1.5 meters onto concrete," thinking about young children dropping the DS and breaking it while playing. Remember that this was during a time where the cell phones that did exist were practically bricks in one's hand.[120]

---

118   "Lifetime Global Unit Sales of Video Game Consoles As of September 2020," Statista, accessed October 1, 2020.

119   Dave Kosak, "Game Developers Rant!," GameSpy, March 16, 2005.

120   · Funnily enough, I dropped my Nintendo DS Lite in 2008 at a height that was barely twelve inches off the ground onto my grandparents' (soft) bamboo flooring in Japan, and it shattered the hinge joint that was known for being the weakest point of the system. It rendered the top screen unable to take any commands, and it took several weeks to be repaired. Perhaps Nintendo should've spent more time on that hinge.

Aside from being a logistical nightmare to figure out how to prevent a computer from breaking at such a high drop and keep such a device affordable *and* portable—"the hardware design team screamed," as Iwata put it—such a request was unheard of at the time.[121]

Iwata wasn't just a successful programmer or a business visionary who understood the industry he worked in like the back of his hand—he was also charismatic and almost mischievous, unusual for Japanese business executives, and a near antithetical persona to that of the former Nintendo of Japan CEO, Yamauchi, who was known for being a smart businessman, yet stern and authoritarian. Iwata was even named in the *Barron's* top thirty CEOs of the year in 2007 due to the successes of the Nintendo Wii and DS near doubling Nintendo's stock price within the year.[122]

He also helped launch "Nintendo Direct" in 2011—a way of presenting Nintendo's latest projects, but often with a fun twist, like a mock kung-fu brawl with Nintendo of America President Reggie Fils-Aimé for E3 2014 in a pre-recorded video bit.[123] This was done as a reaction to the fact that most mainstream gaming press was quite harsh on Nintendo around this time. "Nintendo Direct" would help to cut out the middleman and enable developers to speak "directly" to their audience, the players. In a similar vein, this is the reason

---

121 Martin Robinson, "Satoru Iwata: A Gentle Revolutionary."

122 Jeremy Reimer, "Nintendo Boss Levels up to 'Top 30 CEO'," Ars Technica, March 28, 2007.

123 *Eurogamer*, "Super Smash Bros. - Mii Character Announce Trailer - E3 2014 - Eurogamer," June 10, 2014, video, 2:18.

why gamers in 2011 looked up to Markus Persson's direct communication with players. Iwata also took part in "Iwata Asks," a series in which Iwata interviewed Nintendo's development teams to hear about Nintendo's anecdotal histories of games they had developed for the general public to see.[124]

However, through 2014 and 2015, Iwata was hospitalized twice due to bile duct complications. He passed away due to complications from his tumor on July 11, 2015, at the age of fifty-five.[125] Nintendo announced his passing the following day.[126]

On July 13, 2015, Nintendo headquarters lowered flags to half-staff. Nintendo offices took a moment of silence to honor Iwata. In Kyoto, thousands braved typhoon winds to attend his funeral.[127] In New York City, people from around the world lined up outside the Nintendo store to write messages in a notebook to pay respects.[128]

Fils-Aimé, president of Nintendo of America, said: "Mr. Iwata is gone, but it will be years before his impact on both Nintendo and the full video game industry will be fully

124 Matt Peckham, "Why Nintendo President Satoru Iwata Mattered," *Time*, July 13, 2015.

125 Martin Robinson, "Satoru Iwata: A Gentle Revolutionary."

126 "Notification of Death and Personnel Change of a Representative Director (President)," Nintendo Co., Ltd., July 13, 2015.

127 Brian Crecente, "Thousands Attend Iwata's Funeral in Kyoto," Polygon, July 17, 2015.

128 Samit Sarkar, "A Visit to the Satoru Iwata Memorial at New York's Nintendo World Store," Polygon, July 13, 2015.

appreciated...He always challenged us to push forward...to try the new...to upset paradigms—and most of all, to engage, excite and endear our fans."[129] PlayStation, longtime business competitor of Nintendo, tweeted: "Thank you for everything, Mr. Iwata."[130]

While Iwata was a visionary, he was also an all-around humble, respectful, and kind man who saved enormously large companies from financial failure. The amount of stress that puts on an individual is unimaginable. That he persevered with a smile until the very end shows us what kind of man he was, and what prompted him to leadership roles at HAL Laboratory and Nintendo prove his capability.

As he said during one of his first interfaces with the public: he is a corporate executive, a game developer, and a gamer, and he fulfilled those roles until the very end.

ご冥福をお祈りします。

Rest in peace, Mr. Iwata.

---

129 Luke Plunkett, "The Video Game Community Pays Tribute To Satoru Iwata," Kotaku, July 12, 2015.

130 PlayStation, Twitter post, July 12, 2015, 10:01p.m.

CHAPTER 6

THE MEME CHARM

———

"My name is Reggie. I'm about kicking ass, I'm about taking names, and we're about making games."[131]

—REGGIE FILS-AIMÉ

Did you know that Nintendo of America, the North American branch of Nintendo Co., once seriously considered changing their iconic oval logo to a graffiti one? That's right—in 2002, back when Nintendo faced challenges regarding how to expand their business, one potential solution came up as changing up their logo.[132] Perhaps matching the snarky attitude of Sega, a once major competitor and creator of the *Sonic* franchise, would work. Nintendo of America faced

---

131   *NintendoPro*, "Nintendo E3 2004 Press Conference (Event) - Part 1 of 4," April 13, 2011, video, 15:00.

132   Chris Priestman, "Reggie Fils-Aimé Prevented Nintendo from Having a Graffiti Logo," IGN Entertainment, January 27, 2020.

distinct challenges, separate from the ones faced in Nintendo of Japan by Satoru Iwata.

The company had amassed millions of fans to support their iconic franchises of the 1980s, such as *Super Mario Bros.* (1985), *The Legend of Zelda* (1986), and *Metroid* (1986), but as time pushed forwards into the late '90s and early 2000s, Nintendo had proved themselves reluctant to take risks or make changes. Major gaming press conferences like E3 (Electronic Entertainment Expo) were becoming more live spectacles, with the advent of livestreaming, than a manner of disseminating investor information for shareholders.

Part of the solution was Satoru Iwata being promoted to CEO of the Japanese branch of Nintendo, but Nintendo of America needed somebody more hip, cool, and confident for their brand identity at press conferences and elsewhere.[133] Their conferences at shows like E3 were stale compared to that of their competitors, Microsoft and Sony. The solution? Reginald "Reggie" Fils-Aimé, joining Nintendo of America in 2003 as their executive vice president in sales and marketing and, later, president in 2006.

Fils-Aimé was born in the Bronx of New York City in 1961. He studied at Cornell University to obtain a BS at the Dyson School of Applied Economics and Management and went on to work at companies like Procter & Gamble, Pizza Hut, and MTV in various senior marketing positions. His job at MTV from 2001 to 2003 focused on the twenty-five- to

---

133   Chris Kohler, "How Reggie Fils-Aimé Became a Nintendo Legend," Kotaku, February 22, 2019.

forty-nine-year-old demographic, which proved particularly useful in helping him to understand how to market to a diverse age range of an audience. "That experience was probably one of the major reasons I was recruited by Nintendo in 2003," Fils-Aimé recounted.[134]

He joined Nintendo primarily to help revitalize their brand image to their young audience, and that was just what he did at the 2004 E3 conference. He introduced himself to the industry by saying: "My name is Reggie. I'm about kicking ass, I'm about taking names, and we're about making games."[135]

FUN FACTS:

Games He's Worked On: *Wii Fit* (2007), *Super Smash Bros. for Wii U* (2014)
Companies Worked: Pizza Hut, Guinness Import Company, MTV, Nintendo
Favorite (Nintendo) Game: *The Legend of Zelda* (1986-) series and *Resident Evil* (1996-) series[136]

It was completely out of the blue. Coming from an unknown face of Nintendo of America's executive board, Fils-Aimé's presentation was a stark contrast compared to previous

---

134 Reggie Fils-Aimé, "Life As the Regginator," interview by Bobbi Dempsey, The *New York Times*, November 18, 2007.

135 *NintendoPro*, "Nintendo E3 2004 Press Conference."

136 Kim Peterson, "Putting Nintendo Back in the Game," *The Seattle Times*, November 12, 2006.

Nintendo E3 presentations, which tended to be well-rehearsed and lacking in any entertainment value. He swaggered his way to fame during this presentation; hardcore Nintendo fans began to call him the "Regginator." Just like Iwata's presentation that would soon happen at the GDC in 2005, it was a welcome surprise for much of the Nintendo community.

Conference attendees barely had time to take in what was happening, because then Fils-Aimé pulled out a prototype of the Nintendo DS, the revolutionary device that would go on to be the second best-selling game system of all time. As a spiritual successor to previous handheld devices like the Game Boy and the Game Boy Advance, the DS was both new and familiar.

Along with his bold personality, Nintendo presented a trailer for an unnamed *The Legend of Zelda* game that would later become *The Legend of Zelda: Twilight Princess* (2006) for the GameCube and Wii, another cult classic of the series. "Blades will bleed...shields will shatter," words on the screen declared, while viewers watched Link hack-and-slash through Moblins riding evil-looking, red-eyed boars, and deftly spin his sword before slinging it into his sheath.[137] The audience went wild. It was a demonstration that Nintendo would hold true to their promise by showcasing games that matched the attitude of Fils-Aimé's presentation.

Despite all of this, Fils-Aimé was initially reluctant about the persona. "I was the devil's advocate—is this *really* what we

_____

137 *PlayscopeTimeline*, "The Legend of Zelda - Twilight Princess - Trailer E3 2004 - GameCube.mov," December 27, 2009, video, 1:05.

want to say [to our customers]?" Fils-Aimé recalls asking.[138] He wanted to be sure that this message would get across that Nintendo was providing accessible entertainment for all consumers, unlike Microsoft and Sony's plans to increase hardware capability. He knew that he wasn't really this "bro-ish" type: he was really a normal, albeit outgoing, business executive. Would being so forthright come off as ludicrous or aggressive?

Fils-Aimé's fears were for naught. Nintendo maintained what they'd said: they'd make games for *everyone*, not just hard-core gamers. Iwata ran the behind-the-scenes of the com-pany, while Fils-Aimé would serve as a refreshing change to Nintendo's executive lineup. Microsoft's Xbox had the supe-rior hardware specs, and Sony's PlayStation 2 had a DVD player, both of which the Nintendo GameCube lacked. But Fils-Aimé was going to help revolutionize Nintendo's image through innovative marketing strategies.

That's why, for one, Nintendo released the Wii in 2006 as a home console that focused on accessibility for all ages instead of computing power. The Wii sported a completely new TV remote-like controller, straying away from the common dual-held controllers. It had an additional nunchuck for the play-er's other hand to provide the same amount of controls that traditional controllers had without making the Wii remote too bogged down with buttons. A sensor bar placed nearby the TV had an advanced accelerometer that could sense

---

138 Sam Machkovech, "The Story of How Nintendo's Iconic Logo Escaped an 'Age-Up' Remake," Ars Technica, January 27, 2020.

acceleration in all three axes and therefore provide realistic feedback of the player's hand movements.[139]

Fils-Aimé demonstrated the Wii's add-on devices at expos to increase awareness of these products. His persona and charisma would amplify their exposure. For example, Fils-Aimé demonstrated the Wii Balance Board at E3 in 2007 with Shigeru Miyamoto, Nintendo's famed Japanese game designer. They played a soccer game for the Wii and measured Reggie's BMI: 27.51, it recorded, and Miyamoto commented that ideally it should be 22 for an adult male of his height. "Muscle is heavier than fat," commented Reggie, to the audience's laughter. "Good excuses," Miyamoto responded in turn, in English.[140]

What's important to realize is that none of these moments were scripted.[141] They happened as a product of Fils-Aimé's charisma. Neither Miyamoto nor Fils-Aimé acted like they were in front of an audience of thousands, both in person and digitally, many of whom were there to criticize their business and design decisions and ruin Nintendo's sales. Instead, they acted like two friends hanging out together after office hours. By inviting the audience into an intimate moment, they weren't just "selling products"—they were personifying themselves as *people* before their roles as executives. It's difficult to quantify what an effect this

139   E3 2006, "Outline of Wii," Nintendo co., accessed August 31, 2020, distributed by The Internet Archive Wayback Machine.

140   *Gadgetress*, "Wii BMI Test," July 16, 2007, video, 5:11.

141   *Syed Islam*, "Reggie Fils-Aimé on Memes in Marketing," October 22, 2019, video, 2:16.

had on sales numbers, but from the number of "memes," jokes, and hubbub that surfaces online after these events, it's easy to see the free marketing that happens from such genuine interaction.

Aside from personality-driven branding decisions, Fils-Aimé also worked on innovative strategies on how to market games for the Wii. He supported the decision to package the game *Wii Sports* (2006) with the console. *Wii Sports* was an active "sports" game that would partner well with the Wii Remote, which emphasized getting up off the couch and playing "virtual" sports in your living room. Players could play solo or group sport games such as bowling, tennis, and golf. The game was included in the Americas and in Europe alongside the Wii.[142]

Iwata actually disagreed with Fils-Aimé about whether to include *Wii Sports* alongside the console. They had a potential for significant loss of revenue by including a $40-50 game for free. Fils-Aimé believed that because the Wii and *Wii Sports* targeted the "family" market so heavily, the gains would outweigh the losses. His theory was that parents would be much more willing to buy the console if they knew their children would be more active, unlike with traditional video games.

"We chose to include it…and it was the right call," Fils-Aimé regarded the decision.[143] The Wii, and Wii Sports (2006),

---

142 *Cornell SC Johnson College of Business,* "Reggie Fils-Aimé '83 - Principle 6: Courage In Decision-Making," October 30, 2019, video, 2:15.

143 *Syed Islam,* "Reggie Fils-Aimé on Memes in Marketing."

broke records, selling over eleven million copies and becoming the best-selling Wii game of all time by the end of 2007.[144]

Fils-Aimé continued as CEO of Nintendo of America, achieving great success with the Nintendo Wii and Nintendo DS. It would only be a matter of time, though, before Fils-Aimé would fail to lead Nintendo in the right direction for their newest hardware: the Wii U.

The Wii U flunked, moving only thirteen million lifetime units.[145] In part, this was due to the fact that the Wii U was not fully portable and players could not play apart from the home console next to the TV. This begged the question of why consumers should even bother to buy the Wii U when they already had the Wii, a decent alternative—a similar issue that Nintendo had encountered with the similarity between the DS and the 3DS, its predecessor.

"When we launched Wii U, we missed the opportunity to be clear on the concept, to show off its capabilities and what the users could do. And that hurt us. Sales were also hurt, during the beginning of its lifespan, by the lack of games," Fils-Aimé described later in 2016.[146]

144 *Guinness World Rec Gamers Ed.* (London: Little Brown Books, 2008), digital, distributed by Archive.org.

145 "Dedicated Video Game Sales Units," Investor Relations Information, Nintendo, June 30, 2020.

146 Francisco Aguirre A., "Reggie Fils-Aimé, presidente de Nintendo América: 'Nos Dolió que los Fanáticos No Entendieran a Wii U'" [Reggie Fils-Aimé, President of Nintendo of America: 'It Hurt Us That Fans Didn't Understand Wii U'], *La Tercera*, June 20, 2016.

Fils-Aimé's marketing strategy also assumed that name recognition would serve them well, considering the success of the Wii. So they chose "Wii U." The problem with that, though, was the fact that consumers didn't understand what was different about the Wii and this so-called "Wii U." It didn't appear to have different types of games, different technical capabilities, or a significant hardware upgrade. Some thought it was an add-on to the Wii that allowed for asymmetrical gameplay. So, many brushed it off as some kind of accessory that they didn't need.

After all of this, Nintendo had taken a fiscal beating. Through 2012 to 2014, Nintendo worked at an operating loss.[147] Though Fils-Aimé often appeared with Iwata in the popular and quirky *Nintendo Direct* informational videos, which helped to maintain a healthy relationship with fans, the company's finances were suffering.

Nintendo needed something to revitalize their gaming. They had played it rather safe with the Wii U and 3DS, and another generation of consoles was coming out in the mid- to late-2010s. Nintendo needed a truly revolutionary console if they wanted to stay in the business.

The first announcement came from Iwata in 2015: "Nintendo is currently developing a dedicated game platform with a brand-new concept under the development code-name 'NX.'"[148] Then they officially announced the console

---

147   "Annual Report 2015," Nintendo Co., Ltd, accessed August 31, 2020.

148   Wesley Yin-Poole, "Nintendo NX Is 'New Hardware with a Brand New Concept'," *Eurogamer*, June 5, 2015.

in October 2016 with the name "Nintendo Switch" alongside a trailer that demonstrated the hardware's hybrid nature.[149] It was going to be a "better" Wii U, now with the previously promised portability built in.

This time, Fils-Aimé was sure to clarify Nintendo's pitch. "We've been incredibly clear with the positioning of the [Switch]," Fils-Aimé described in an interview with *The Star*.[150] "Why should you purchase this device? Well, it's because you can play this great content, anywhere, anytime with anyone. Tell me what the Wii U proposition was in ten words or less. We weren't as incredibly clear."

It's true: when you go back and look at some of the Wii U ads, many of them clearly say, "Upgrade to the Wii U for $299.99," not "Purchase the Wii U for $299.99."[151] This distinction between *"upgrade"* and *"purchase"* confused consumers. But with the Switch, Nintendo was clear to showcase in advertisements that players could bring the Switch with them to the airport like a DS, play it on the TV with a full-on controller, or play it on the go, with the handles of the Switch separated from the screen.[152] This helped consumers realize this was a new, innovative machine that they'd be willing to spend $299.99 on.

149   Aaron Souppouris, "'Switch' is Nintendo's Next Game Console," Engadget, October 20, 2016.

150   Raju Mudhar, "E3 Interview With Nintendo's Reggie Fils-Aimé: What's So Special About Canadian Videogamers?," *The Star*, June 15, 2018.

151   *StevoniStuffThings*, "The Very Bad Wii U Ads," July 6, 2017, video, 6:47.

152   *Nintendo*, "First Look at Nintendo Switch," October 20, 2016, video, 3:37.

Another upgrade Fils-Aimé commented on was adding a larger library for the Nintendo Switch. "Whether it's the big companies like Electronic Arts, or whether it's the smaller independent developer, we need those companies to create content to support us. We have that now with Nintendo Switch."[153] Instead of relying on mostly first-party games made by development teams affiliated with Nintendo, this time, Nintendo could work with third-party, unaffiliated developers to bring more games to the Switch. It was a new marketing strategy for Nintendo, which traditionally strays away from non-affiliated developers, and was one advocated for by Fils-Aimé.

To market the Switch, Fils-Aimé went live with Jimmy Fallon (alongside Shigeru Miyamoto, yet again) to give the public their very first look at the Nintendo Switch and *The Legend of Zelda: Breath of the Wild* (2017). Fallon, who has mass market appeal to almost every demographic, helped show off the Switch with equal parts nerves and excitement. "I'm geeking out—I'm geeking out right now!" stutter-shouted an excited Fallon as Fils-Aimé removed a Question Mark Block box off to reveal the Nintendo Switch.[154]

He started off by giving Fallon a brief demonstration of *Breath of the Wild*. Fils-Aimé handled Fallon's "geeking out" outbursts with smooth charm, easily rolling his comments into more knowledge he shared about the Switch. He

153 Damien McFerran, "Wii U's Failure Is Responsible for Switch's Success, Says Reggie," Nintendo Life, November 10, 2016.

154 *The Tonight Show Starring Jimmy Fallon*, "Jimmy Fallon Debuts the Nintendo Switch," December 7, 2016, video, 9:40.

amazed the audience the most, though, when he switched off from the Nintendo Switch Pro controller he had been using (which looks just like a traditional controller) to use the Nintendo Switch as a portable console. "It's three consoles in one console!...Every kid, every human, every person will be playing with this, come March!" exclaimed Fallon.[155]

The "Switch" approach worked: the Switch has since sold fifty-five million units and 356 million software units, significantly better than the Wii U's thirteen million and 103 million software units.[156]

It was the unfortunate passing of Satoru Iwata, his coworker and dear friend, in 2015 that inspired Fils-Aimé to think about the legacy he would leave at Nintendo. Iwata's passing reminded him of how fleeting life is, and it made him think about how he could prepare for his own retirement from Nintendo. "That event certainly crystallized for me the importance and motivated me to be clear and intentional in what I wanted to do."[157]

On April 15, 2019, Fils-Aimé retired from his position as Chief Operating Officer of Nintendo. He rode Nintendo through its success with the Nintendo Wii and Switch, and stayed in spite of the failures of the Wii U. Still, some of the biggest takeaways from his tenure may come from his disposition toward his job and how a business executive may still joke

---

155   Ibid.

156   Investor Relations Information, "Message from the President."

157   James Brightman, "[Exclusive] Reggie Fils-Aimé."

around with consumers without coming off as out-of-touch or tacky.

YouTube is rife with compilations of Fils-Aimé's presentations, where he acts like a robot version of himself in "Reggie Fils-A-Mech," trains on the weightlifting bench by counting to "Nintendo...sixty-three, Nintendo...sixty-four," and tells the Super Smash Bros champion at the 2014 *Super Smash Bros.* Invitational that he'll "kick his ass."[158] That is part of what has built up his persona in a way that was relatable with players, instead of feeling tacky or pretentious.

"The memes I [and Mr. Iwata and Mr. Miyamoto] were a part of...creates a relationship with our consumer and having a healthy relationship with our customer drives sales," Fils-Aimé explained during his Cornell lecture. In spite of the fact that he—or let's say, his body—was not ready for each meme, he stated that he believes his personality and the passion he has for the business are what fans responded so well to. "It's not something that you can forcibly create. These memes happen."[159]

Fils-Aimé will be missed for his contributions as Nintendo of America's president. He showed us that business owners didn't have to be corporate or overly polite. They can

158 *Nintendo*, "Reggie Fils-A-Mech - Announcing Nintendo @ E3 2014,"
     April 29, 2014, video, 5:02; *Nintendo*, "Nintendo Digital Event," September
     14, 2015, video, 48:25; *Nintendo*, "Reggie Fils-Aimé Full Speech (Super
     Smash Bros. Invitational 2014)," June 11, 2014, video, 6:21.
159 *Syed Islam*, "Reggie Fils-Aimé on Memes in Marketing."

be fun and engaging, and that the persona of a business executive can revitalize the image of a company. It was exactly what Nintendo needed at the time, and he fulfilled that role aptly.

PART 2

WORKING FOR
A DEVELOPER

CHAPTER 7

ALL WORK, ALL PLAY

"I used to draw cartoons. I'd just show them to some of my friends, expecting that they were going to appreciate them, that they were going to enjoy reading them. And I haven't changed a bit about that. When I'm making video games today, I want people to be entertained. I am always thinking, 'How are people going to enjoy playing the games we are making today?' And as long as I can enjoy something other people can enjoy it, too."[160]

—SHIGERU MIYAMOTO

At this point in the book, we've well covered the different types of leadership that exist in the game development industry, as well as what kind of qualities and decisions go into becoming a leader. In this section of the book, I'd like to shift

---

160 Nick Paumgarten, "Master of Play," *The New Yorker*, December 13, 2010.

gears to how we can persevere as employees in the gaming industry. Just what kind of qualities are required of employees? How do we catch the eyes of employers to hire us?

Shigeru Miyamoto is the sometimes-goofy Japanese video game designer and (later) game director at Nintendo. He's been heralded with being the father of the *Super Mario Brothers* and *The Legend of Zelda* series, two of Nintendo's most successful franchises whose fan bases stay loyal to this day.

It all started in Miyamoto's childhood: born in 1952, he was a boy of modest upbringing in the rural town of Sonobe, Japan. One of his favorite hobbies was to explore his backyard and the woods beyond. He bushwhacked his way through a bamboo forest behind the town's ancient Shinto shrine when he was seven or eight years old. He eventually started to travel far distances by foot or bike to find his next adventure.

There is one particular cave, though, which he refers back to often as a tipping point of discovering a fascination for exploration and a source for inspiration for the many games he has created to date. At first, he approached the cave in the middle of the woods with trepidation. It was just a strange, dark little hole in the grass, after all. But after repeated visits, curiosity overwhelmed Miyamoto. He brought a lantern to venture into the small hole in the ground. What he found was a large network of caverns, which he could explore to his heart's content.

It was this childlike wonder and persistence with which Miyamoto pursued discovery that he applied to his job search as he grew older. Initially he wanted to be a manga artist—a storyteller.[161] He loved the classic Disney characters and he carved his own wooden puppets with his grandfathers' tools. That led him to pursue a college degree in art; in 1976, at age twenty-four, he graduated from the Kanazawa College of Art with a degree in industrial design and a desire to create stories and characters through manga.[162]

At first, Miyamoto was confused as to what he could do. He liked to play bluegrass on the banjo and the guitar, and he liked creating toys and drawing. But he had no job lined up. So, his father got him an interview with Yamauchi, the then-president of Nintendo. Miyamoto showed some examples of toys he'd made, and Yamauchi hired him in 1977 to be an apprentice in the planning department.[163]

When Miyamoto started working at Nintendo, he was originally hired to design a coin-operated arcade game cabinet. At the time, arcade games like *Space Invaders* (1978) were a massive hit among children (as well as a huge moneymaker). Nintendo had created one called *Radarscope*, and it was a failure, selling only one thousand of the three thousand manufactured cabinets.[164] Miyamoto's job was to design a new cabinet and make sure the repurposed cabinets would compensate for the losses.

161 Paumgarten, "Master of Play."

162 Seth Schiesel, "Resistance Is Futile," *The New York Times*, May 25, 2008.

163 Paumgarten, "Master of Play."

164 Marc Nix, "IGN Presents: The History of Super Mario Bros.," IGN Entertainment, September 17, 2015.

"When there is a game that is not yet interesting, I have to think about how I can change it or adjust it so that people can be entertained," Miyamoto explained about his approach to making games.[165] *Radarscope* was a failure, but *why* was it a failure? It was a forced perspective angle of *Space Invaders*, essentially. Perhaps it was just that it was a copy of a popular game that came off as tacky, or that it was hard to play. Either way, Miyamoto would have to reinvent Nintendo's approach to the arcade entirely.

He came up with *Donkey Kong*, released in 1981. The game features Jumpman, an Italian plumber whose pet gorilla has fallen in love with his girlfriend, kidnapped her, and run off to a construction area. (This is actually the first instance of Mario, before the *Super Mario Brothers* series.) Jumpman must jump over and dodge the gorilla's attacks to save his girlfriend.

At first, Nintendo of America executives looked at the game and thought: "We're screwed." The name "Donkey Kong," which Miyamoto had created by translating "Goofy" and "Gorilla" in the Japanese-English dictionary to get "Donkey" and "Kong," respectively, sounded silly, and the premise was outlandish. They at least insisted on changing "Jumpman" to a name like "Mario."[166]

Despite the unusual premise of the game, it was surprisingly addictive in arcades. Nintendo sold sixty-seven thousand cabinets over the next two years—a marked success from

---

165 Paumgarten, "Master of Play."

166 Ibid.

Radarscope.[167] Miyamoto was praised for his work, and Nintendo asked him to continue to create similar genius characters and game design, but this time for the "home market:" console-based video games instead of arcade games.

The early 1980s were a tumultuous time for gaming. Atari, a video game development company, was selling the Atari 2600 (originally called the Atari Video Computer System) as the first home video game console system to break through into mainstream culture. By 1982, though, the video game development market was enormously saturated: tons of games were getting made through third-party developers, but supply was not meeting demand.[168]

FUN FACTS:
Games He's Worked On: *Super Mario Bros.* (1985), *The Legend of Zelda* (1986), *The Legend of Zelda: Breath of the Wild* (2017)
Companies Worked: Nintendo
Favorite Games: *Splatoon (2015), Super Mario Maker (2015)*[169]

Newspapers of the time blamed "consumer boredom" and guessed a crash would happen after Christmas of 1982

---

167 Zev Borow, "Why Nintendo Won't Grow Up," *Wired*, January 1, 2003.

168 Robert Snowdon Jones, "Home Video Games Are Coming under a Strong Attack," *Cox News Service*, December 12, 1982.

169 Mike Futter, "Shigeru Miyamoto Discusses His Favorite Movie and Games of 2015," Game Informer, March 4, 2016.

because large retail stores would realize how many video games they had left unsold in inventory. Brands like Atari and Intellivision, which controlled 80 percent of the market at the time, would suffer the most, they guessed.

The crash came in 1983. Industry analysts had been right; overproduction and lack of consumer trust had realized this issue. No connection existed between the outer appearance of the box and the actual game. Consumers were fooled into promises of a great game because of pretty box art countless times, when the actual game inside was terrible quality. Through 1985, video game industry revenue dropped from $3.2 billion in 1983 to $100 million by 1985.[170] Atari, Inc. closed in 1984, its company fractured. Many analysts doubted that the industry would survive at all.[171] Large retail stores set away the dedicated spaces for video game displays and replaced them with other types of toys, some not selling video games at all.

Nintendo, in spite of this tragedy, wanted to overcome the crash by proving themselves: they would use a certified "Official Nintendo Seal of Quality" to prove that their games stood up to rigorous standards, unlike Atari's highly unregulated, non-standardized third-party developer process.[172] And even if large retail stores had outright banned the selling of video games, Nintendo came up with workarounds: market their

170   Yuji Nakamura, "Peak Video Game? Top Analyst Sees Industry Slumping in 2019," *Bloomberg News*, January 23, 2019.

171   Jones, "Home Video Games."

172   Susan Arendt, "Civilization Creator Lists Three Most Important Innovations in Gaming," *Wired*, Condé Nast, March 4, 2008.

newest console, the Famicom ("Family Computer") as the "Nintendo Entertainment System" (NES), not a console or home computer, like many of Atari's systems branded themselves as. They included a toy robot, "R.O.B.," to convince toy retailers to allow their products in stores at all.[173]

Nintendo had a hidden arsenal, too: a series of talented designers and creatives who simply did not exist in other companies that focused entirely on the programming-side. Shigeru Miyamoto, who had designed *Donkey Kong*, would be among them.

Super Mario Bros (1985) would be the catalyst that would reinvigorate the game industry to what it once was. It would be a game about that same, stereotypical image of an Italian plumber, chasing after his girlfriend, now "Princess Peach," who was in the hands of an evil "Bowser," a giant turtle-like monster with spikes on his shell. It would be a 2-D side-scrolling game.

"I always try to be conscious about...gradual improvement," Miyamoto has described about his game design.[174] With *Mario*, Miyamoto set about to change many norms of game design up until that point. The game would be simple, with only twenty or so items the player could collect to influence gameplay. He would let complexity arise from the simplicity of the game mechanics.

173   Sean O'Kane, "7 Things I Learned from the Designer of the NES," *The Verge*, October 18, 2015.

174   Paumgarten, "Master of Play."

It was the first game ever created to feature a map with a distinction between the "overworld" and "levels." It even came with a catchy music score, the first ever in a video game.[175] The game went on to sell over forty million copies for the original NES, and was actually bundled with the NES itself; in some places, the infamous *Duck Hunt* (1985) came packaged with *Mario* in a "NES action set." It would be the best-selling game of all-time for twenty years afterward.[176]

Miyamoto wasn't done. In 1986, he worked with Nintendo to develop *The Legend of Zelda*. This time, the game would be about a fantasy land, where an elf-like boy called Link would collect the eight fragments of the Triforce of Wisdom to rescue Princess Zelda from an evil king named Ganon.

Unlike *Mario*, *The Legend of Zelda* was top-down, over-world-based, with many puzzles the player would have to solve. The world would be called Hyrule, "a miniature garden that you can put into a drawer and revisit anytime you like," as Miyamoto described.[177]

The game was an ode to the discovery that Miyamoto loved as a child: by venturing into nondescript caves from the over-world map, the player could discover entire stories, characters, and monsters, like those Miyamoto had fantasized about as a child.

---

175   Borow, "Why Nintendo Won't Grow Up."

176   Keith Stuart, "Super Mario Bros: 25 Mario Facts for the 25th Anniversary," *The Guardian*, September 13, 2010, distributed by The Internet Archive Wayback Machine.

177   Paumgarten, "Master of Play."

Over four decades later, he is now the senior management director and general manager of the Entertainment Analysis and Development division at Nintendo Company Ltd. Miyamoto became famous both by personality and by talent. He pauses before answering questions to think and he responds in paragraphs.[178] Above all, he's known for the constant goofy smile he wears, unlike the custom in Japan to remain polite and professional at all times.

He refers to himself as the *ningen kougaku*, or "human engineer," of Nintendo.[179] When asked about designing games, he says, "It's about enjoying something...I used to draw cartoons. I'd just show them to some of my friends, expecting that they were going to appreciate them...and I haven't changed a bit about that. When I'm making video games today, I want people to be entertained."[180] In this way, Miyamoto is always thinking about how to make people happy while playing games.

Miyamoto also described what has helped him create games at Nintendo. "Sometimes I ask the younger game creators to try playing the games they are making by switching their left and right hands," he explained to Sheff of *The New Yorker*. "In that way, they can understand how inexperienced the first-timer is."[181] And Nintendo doesn't use focus groups. Instead, Miyamoto thinks to himself about how best to entertain

---

178 Ibid.
179 Ibid.
180 Ibid.
181 Ibid.

players, while remaining empathetic in how difficult they view the game.

Miyamoto's ingenuity and charm have helped him become an icon in game design. Holding his child-like curiosity close by his side has led him to success as a designer.

CHAPTER 8

LIFE IN MOTION

———

"I really like to capture movement. I really like the concept that what you're seeing is not just a flat painting of something. It's really a moment, even if it's 2-D, captured from one point to the other."

—INGRID SANASSEE

The first time Ingrid Sanassee touched a computer, she was nine years old. Having grown up on Mauritius, a tropical island far from the coasts of Madagascar, she struggled with access to the technology she wanted. Mauritius ranks "high" in the Human Development Index of the United Nations that ranks countries based on life expectancy, education, and per capita income, and is a developing country with an average per capita gross domestic product of $10,949.[182] Back in the '90s when Sanassee was a young girl, having a computer was

———

182 "GDP Per Capita (Constant 2010 US$) - Mauritius," The World Bank Group, accessed September 16, 2019.

like owning a Maserati. And luckily enough, her cousin managed to get his hands on one, with several games on it to boot.

She was transfixed the first time she played games like *Wolfenstein* and *Doom*. The game that amazed her most, though, was *Tomb Raider* (1993). *Tomb Raider* was iconic for its time; in a time where games were all-out action with guns and a male lead, a stealth-based heroine hunting for ancient treasures was quite rare. And to top it all off, the game was in 3-D.

The way the 3-D graphics, animations, and world looked "like magic," Sanassee said to me in our interview. She remembers the night she beat the game, mesmerized by the names on the credits screen as they went by. That night she told her mother she wanted to make video games. "That's good, that's good… Now finish your mashed potatoes," her mother replied.[183]

Sanassee also loved movement. She loved dance since a young age (particularly ballet and African dance), and for that reason too, *Tomb Raider* caught her eye, in which the main character is highly acrobatic. "For me, dance is the expression that represents all the possible movement a body can do," she describes. "Each move has to be so precise, and… choreographed and prepared in a specific way to express the big picture."[184] She became obsessed with animation and its ability to express the movements of the human body. That

---

183 "Quantic Dream & Me - Interview with Ingrid, Motion Kit Lead," Quantic Dream, October 31, 2019.

184 Ibid.

chasm between dance in real life and movement in video games was bridged by animation.

At first, Sanassee didn't think she *could* work in the video game industry. "Video games, for me, were at the top, the very top," she said. She just wanted to get her foot in the door any way she could—and she didn't know if she could even get *in* to the video game industry. Finding somewhere to work in 3-D animation was already difficult enough on Mauritius, where no colleges nor studios employed 3-D animators.

Until 2001, that is. It was just after Sanassee received her certificate in arts and mathematics from Queen Elisabeth College in Mauritius. She was browsing the local newspaper when she found an ad that declared a famous French 3-D animation studio, Gribouille, was opening a branch in Mauritius named TropikAnim. They were looking for candidates to train and hire for their art and animation team. Specifically, they wanted artists to work on motion capture.

Motion capture was a new technology at the time that functioned as a way to get physical acting into animation for film or video games. Unlike computer graphics-based animation, motion capture does what it says—it literally captures motion from a person's movements in the physical world.[185*] Markers are placed all over the actor's body, and the actors'

---

185 * Computer graphics-based animation, or keyframe animation, is the traditional way animators animate when motion capture is unavailable. Using 3-D modeling/animation programs, animators create a skeleton of a character and set "keyframes," or points of importance, where the character's arm moves during a "walk" animation.

movements are tracked by the markers on computer software. These points are saved as movement vectors, each assigned a skeletal component such as "left arm" or "right foot." These animation vectors are then laid over the model of a cartoon character, for example, to use the captured motion as digital animation. Gribouille was one of the first studios to use Motion Capture technology in a TV show to create animations for *Xcalibur*, a children's fantasy show.[186]

If Sanassee didn't apply then, she didn't know if she'd ever have a chance again. She didn't have formal training in 3-D animation, but she pushed herself to apply, citing her arts and mathematics background. TropikAnim were training candidates on the job, after all. And just like that, she found her way in.

Sanassee continued to work at TropikAnim through 2002. It was that year, though, when the TropikAnim branch closed. Some members of the company offered Sanassee to follow the French team back to France to continue working there. Language was not a problem—Mauritians speak English, French, and French-based Creole, or some combination of the three. So she followed her "European dream" to head to south of France to work at Gribouille.

There, she found that she had a growing desire to learn. She wanted to teach herself as much as she could about animation, interactive programming, and interactivity in general. It would be the start of her journey of self-taught game development, a topic she is a major advocate of.

---

186 Ibid.

So, in 2002, she decided to start her own venture, on top of pursuing a degree in arts at the University of Provence. She partnered with Pascal Lefort, an artist with whom she had previously worked, to cofound PakingProd, where she acted as codirector and web designer. She explored many different multimedia art forms: cartoons, artistic films, and web design for companies such as Ubisoft and artists such as Kolkoz. She taught herself web development languages like HTML, CSS, and JavaScript to be able to mix interactivity with her job.

Sanassee built her resume and expanded out from just 3-D animation. At the end of the day, it was all a means to an end of exploring interactivity—if you can think of web development as a study of the users' movement in the same way ballet is a study of physical movement.

By July of 2006, Sanassee's hard work paid off. She was hired by Ubisoft to work on *Beowulf: The Game* (2007) as a 3-D Animator. Finally, she could realize her largest aspiration: animations for video games! However, at release, *Beowulf* was met with mixed reviews at best, such as Gamespot stating, "Even a merry band of adventurous thanes can't save this quest from ruin."[187]

Sanassee moved on to *I AM ALIVE* (2012) at Darkworks, working with Ubisoft as its publisher, in 2007 as a lead animator. This time, the game was much more successful, selling somewhere between two hundred thousand to five

---

187   Joe Dodson, "Beowulf: The Game Review," GameSpot, CBS Interactive Inc, November 21, 2007.

hundred thousand copies.[188] Most important of all, Sanassee learned rigging, facial animation, and motion capture pipeline like the back of her hand. And soon, it would *really* pay off.

It was in November 2011 when Sanassee found herself in the position of senior animator at Quantic Dream, the studio owned by David Cage that released *Heavy Rain* in February 2010. At the time, *Heavy Rain* (2010) was putting Quantic Dream in the video game industry spotlight, both for its unexpectedly high sales numbers, interactive story, and technical innovations. For Sanassee, being able to work at Quantic Dream was a big deal.

Because Quantic Dream makes their own game engine for every game, and because every game is a new IP (they do not make sequels), this often results in games that maximize the console for which it is developed. At the time, their latest game, *Heavy Rain,* was being praised for its realistic facial movements and acting through motion capture. Funded by their newest publisher, Sony, there was quite a lot of money behind the technology, too. It was a perfect hotbed for Sanassee's skills.

At Quantic Dream, Sanassee started working on *Beyond: Two Souls*, set to release in October 2013. Her years of diligent work in 3-D animation, motion capture, and integrating these all into video games paid off.

---

188 "I Am Alive," Steam Spy, Steam, accessed August 24, 2020.

Something I was curious about with motion capture technology is how accurately an actor's movements translate to a computer 3-D animation/modeling software like Blender or Maya. Sanassee told me about motion capture animation: "If the actor is not good, the animation won't be good."

FUN FACTS:

Games She's Worked On: *I AM ALIVE* (2012), *Beowulf: The Game* (2007), *Beyond: Two Souls* (2013), *Detroit: Become Human* (2018)

Companies Worked: TropikAnim, Ubisoft, Darkworks, Pakingprod, Quantic Dream

Game she would like to create with infinite resources: A game created using skills learned by self-taught developers.

Favorite Games: *Journey* (2012), *Shadow of Colossus* (2005), *Gris* (2018) *Tomb Raider* (1993), *Wolfenstein 3D* (1992)

When the actor enters the "Volume," or the room where motion capture happens, they are often initially struck by its sparseness. The room is completely black, with hundreds of cameras pointing at the central floor of the room. Colorful tape lines the floor where actors are expected to act. Combined with the fact that the actor wears a black skin-tight body suit with gray markers the size of golf balls all over their body, it can be overwhelming for those who have never done motion capture before (many of the actors that David Cage hires for his games hadn't, simply because motion capture for games in the early 2010's was unusual).

Pascal Langdale, the motion capture actor for Ethan Mars in *Heavy Rain*, recounted his experience working on the *Heavy Rain* set on an Inaugural Quantic Dream Livestream on May 25, 2020: "If you are physically unbelievable, meaning you are not in character...then it will show."[189][190]*

For *Beyond: Two Souls*, Quantic Dream even managed to hire Ellen Page, an up-and-coming popular actor from shows and movies like *Inception* (2010) and *To Rome With Love* (2012). Others included Willem Dafoe and Eric Winter. Sanassee would be able to put her skills to good use with talented actors. "We don't want actors to exaggerate their movements one bit...At Quantic Dream, we want natural [movement]," Sanassee emphasized.

Beyond: Two Souls, released in 2013, went on to sell one million copies in its first two months of sales and also became one of the best-selling games for the PS3. Its motion capture and facial animations were much improved since *Heavy Rain*, with reviewers praising it: *PlayStation Official Magazine* (UK) called *Beyond* the "PS3's graphical high point" and *Polygon* saying, "staggeringly great" motion capture.[191] Compare

---

189   "Temps fort : Inaugural Quantic Dream Livestream,"Quantic Dream, video, 2:47:51, May 25, 2020.

190   * Langdale now teaches motion capture to young, aspiring artists due to his love for the craft.

191   Phil Iwaniuk, "Beyond: Two Souls Review – an Essential Purchase for Interactive-Drama Fans," Official PlayStation Magazine UK, October 8, 2013, distributed by The Internet Archive Wayback Machine; Justin McElroy, "Beyond Two Souls Review: Hand in Hand, "Polygon, October 8, 2013, distributed by The Internet Archive Wayback Machine.

that to Quantic Dream's newest hit, *Detroit: Become Human* (2018), a game about androids living amongst humans, that went on to move one million copies in just two weeks.

As of 2019, Sanassee has since been promoted to lead motion kit animation. This means she oversees the motion capture projects at Quantic Dream, from making sure actors' movements are properly captured and that those animations look good in-game. Nowadays, she doesn't work as much on the actual animations herself. "Even if I don't touch the mouse... everything is in [my] head," she admitted.

Having worked on motion capture for video games for so many years, I was curious about her process. Is motion capture animation that different from traditional keyframe animation? To my surprise, she answered that motion capture is basically the same as keyframe animation from an end-result standpoint.

The actor's performance, she emphasized, is the make-or-break of character animations in motion capture. Aside from this fact, animators still have to touch up a motion capture's body movements after it is shot. "Motion capture can make the animation feel heavy," Sanassee explained. While we're used to playing games where the main character snaps into a walk cycle or jumps into the air with their arms fully extended upwards, the animations captured in motion capture feel "slow." And if you're wondering why, it's because even the most talented of actors are, well, human—not fictional video game characters. Yes, even the most average of video game characters is blessed with the superpower of being able to jerk into a sprint in less than a second.

Sanassee's passion for observing movement in-game has translated into real-life. She'll watch a coworker walk down the hall, and simply based on the movement of their shoulders, knees, or head, she can tell if they're walking in a way that's compensating for neck pain or for ankle pain. Imagine how jealous a physical therapist would be.

Aside from her time at Quantic Dream, though, she practices self-taught programming, art, game design, and audio. "[I want] to make people see that it's not impossible to make your own [games], even when you know nothing," she explained. Much of how she got to where she is now, from web development to animation, was all self-taught.

If Sanassee wants young game developers to know one thing, it's that self-taught game development (or any topic, for that matter) *is* possible.

Sanassee came from a background where, unless she pushed herself to learn on her own, she would not have reached where she is today. Not only that, but she applied herself to potentially uncomfortable job interviews to move forward in her desired career direction. To succeed in the game industry in the field we desire, whether it be programming or art or design, we must apply ourselves with the same amount of ambition demonstrated by Sanassee to realize our full potential.

CHAPTER 9

WHEN LIGHTNING STRIKES

———

"This is an industry in which you constantly have to relearn things and almost start over. If you can't do that, you don't last."[192]

—AMY HENNIG

Amy Hennig, an American video game director and screenwriter, never planned on working in the video game industry. When she was thirteen years old in 1977, *Star Wars Episode IV* released in theaters, the Atari 2600 console was released, and *Advanced Dungeons & Dragons* was ready to play. Yet despite having interest in gaming from a young age and enjoying the process of learning about the stories behind

———

192 Ben Fritz, "How I Made It: Amy Hennig," *Los Angeles Times*, February 7, 2010.

the games, the spark for working in the game development industry wouldn't light until much, much later.

When Hennig went to college at the University of California, Berkeley, in 1982, she decided to pursue a bachelor's degree in English. She moved onto a master's program in film theory and production in 1989. Just as a side hustle during film school, Hennig took up a freelance job as an artist for *Electrocop* (1989), a game for the Atari 7800 system. There, she worked as a designer and animator, working with just four color samples to draw the art. "It was purely for pay," Hennig explained in an interview with the *LA Times*. "But once I started, my wheels began to turn and I had a lightbulb moment: that this was a more interesting and pioneering medium than film."[193] She placed herself where lighting struck and took off running.

Because she found working on *Electrocop's* art and game design so compelling, she dropped out of film school in 1991 to focus on video game production and artwork.[194] In that same year, Hennig managed to get a job at Electronic Arts (EA) as a game designer and artist. At EA, she worked as an artist for *Desert Strike: Return to the Gulf* (1992) for the Sega Genesis, as well as for *Bard's Tale IV* (never released). On each of these games, Hennig refined her game design and art principle skills.

It was in 1993, though, that Hennig was given an opportunity to shine. She was working on a game called *Michael Jordan:*

---

193   Ibid.

194   "Amy Hennig," LinkedIn Corporation, accessed August 25, 2020.

Chaos in the Windy City (1994). The lead designer for the project quit, and they needed a replacement. The team needed to look no further than Hennig herself, who had proven herself to have an eye for design.

This was a big break for Hennig. After risking a potentially rewarding career in film for games, the game development fuse was lit.

In 1995, Hennig moved onto working at Crystal Dynamics as the in a more managerial position on the *Legacy of Kain/ Soul Reaver* series. She first worked with Silicon Knights, a now-defunct Canadian game development company to work on *Blood Omen: Legacy of Kain* (1996), and then moved on to games like *Legacy of Kain: Soul Reaver* (1999) during which she worked as the director, producer, and writer. She did similar work on *Soul Reaver 2* (2001) and *Legacy of Kain: Defiance* (2003).

In spite of all of the previous impressive positions she was working in, her greatest step into the spotlight was yet to come. In 2003, she left Crystal Dynamics to start work at Naughty Dog, where she was initially tasked with the *Jak and Daxter* series, but soon moved on as a creative director and lead writer on a new game, *Uncharted: Drake's Fortune* (2007). *Uncharted* was going to be a game about Nathan Drake, the supposed descendant of Sir Francis Drake, a famous English explorer of the Elizabethan era.

From the moment *Uncharted* was announced at E3 2006, its plot was compared to *Tomb Raider,* even going so far as to call the game "Dude Raider." Naughty Dog wanted the story and Nathan Drake to be completely different, though; instead of *Tomb Raider*'s puzzle-based gameplay, they wanted a stealth-based game and character. "[Drake]'s not a ninja, Special Forces guy," said Richard Lemarchand, lead game designer on the project. "He's constantly living on the edge of his abilities."[195]

This was no thanks to Hennig, who also received help from Lemarchand himself, Neil Druckmann, another game designer, and Josh Scherr, lead cinematic animator, in writing Drake's character. "The creative environment at Naughty Dog is very open," said Lemarchand in an interview with IGN, "and every last member of our team is unique, and finds its own way of rolling the story's writers into the process."[196]

Funnily enough, when asked about whether Naughty Dog might've made Nathan Drake a woman along the same lines of Lara Croft, Hennig completely denied the possibility. "We already got criticized for...Dude Raider," she said in an interview with *VentureBeat*. "It would feel like we were invading [*Tomb Raider's*] territory. She was this aspirational, acrobatic James Bond character, so we made ours a little hapless, a little clumsy, more like Harrison Ford in Indiana Jones."[197]

---

195   "Dude Raiders," The Sydney Morning Herald, October 4, 2007, distributed by The Internet Archive Wayback Machine.

196   Michael Thomsen, "Inside the Story: Naughty Dog Interview," IGN, May 12, 2012.

197   Dean Takahashi, "Amy Hennig Interview — Surviving the Trauma of Making a Video Game and Inspiring Newcomers," Venture Beat, February 22, 2019.

While *Uncharted* was delayed many times during development due to having to build a new game engine for the PS3, game design, and plot in-cohesion, it eventually released in 2007 to highly favorable reviews. It received IGN's award of PlayStation 3 game of the year.[198] By the time 2009 rolled around, *Uncharted* had sold over 2.6 million copies globally.[199] And in 2008, Naughty Dog announced they would create a sequel to the game.

On *Uncharted 2: Among Thieves*, Hennig's oversight at Naughty Dog grew while still working as a writer for the game. On her team were 150 people including programmers, actors, and game designers. To supply that work demand, the game came with a budget of $20 million—the same as for its prequel. The money saved by not having to develop a new engine would come from working on including a richer narrative and more content.[200]

Hennig found that working on the *Uncharted* games were shaping up to be more like her career in film than she'd expected. Setting up cutscenes, like fights on top of moving trains and shootouts in open fields, were oddly familiar to her. "Everything I learned as an undergraduate with English literature and in film school about editing and shots and the

---

198 "Best of 2007," IGN Entertainment, accessed August 25, 2020.

199 Tor Thorsen, "PS3 Motion Controller Revealed, God of War III Due in March," GameSpot, June 2, 2009, distributed by The Internet Archive Wayback Machine.

200 Robert Purchese, "Uncharted Sequel to Cost USD 20 Million," Eurogamer, February 5, 2009.

language of film has come into play, but in a way I couldn't possibly have planned," she described.[201]

FUN FACTS:

Companies Worked: EA, Crystal Dynamics, Naughty Dog, Skydance

Games She's Worked On: *Uncharted: Drake's Fortune* (2007), *Uncharted 2: Among Thieves* (2009)

The concept of cutscenes is an in-game sequence that is not interactive; it acts just like a clip of a film, where the player watches the events that happen. Cutscenes can set the mood, show conversations between two characters, or give a cinematic overview of the surroundings.

The earliest cutscenes, like those as simple as the ones in *Pac-Man* (1980) demonstrating the effect of the Energizer power pellet power-up, while those of today rival the cinematography of real films. When Hennig joined Naughty Dog, cutscenes had featured human characters for a couple of years prior, and so she had resources to work with to make cutscenes imitate the films that she had nearly worked on.

As production for *Uncharted 2: Among Thieves* progressed, fans began to wonder: who exactly was the mastermind behind the plot and these characters? It was during this time that Hennig's name began to attract attention. The attention was almost all positive.

---

201 Ben Fritz, "How I Made It."

Having your works become successful often comes with a price: fame. Though Hennig had been relatively unknown up until this point, with many interviews before 2007 excluding any mentions of her except her name, that began to change during the development of *Uncharted 2* through 2009.

"It's mostly nice, because a lot of young people come up to me, game designers, who will say they got into this because of me," she told Dean Takahashi from *VentureBeat* in February 2019. "That makes everything worth it."[202] Still, Hennig prefers to stay out of the spotlight, declining to discuss details of controversies or interpersonal issues.

Uncharted 2 was released in October 2009 and, like its predecessor, also came out to high accolades, receiving several "Game of the Year" awards and receiving an extremely rare Metacritic score of 96 out of 100.[203] *Naughty Dog* would soon announce a third to the now-trilogy, called *Uncharted 3: Drake's Deception*, which would go on to release in 2011.[204]

Though things looked great from the outside, that wasn't the case from the inside. When *Uncharted 3* was being developed, there was another project—*The Last of Us* (2013)—being developed alongside it. And this was causing "crunch:" a

---

202 Dean Takahashi, "Amy Hennig Interview."

203 Evan Wells, "Uncharted 2 Takes Game of the Year at VGAs — behind the Scenes with Naughty Dog's Evan Wells," PlayStation Blog, December 18, 2009, distributed by The Internet Archive Wayback Machine; "Uncharted 2: Among Thieves," Metacritic, October 13, 2009.

204 Jeff Rubenstein, "Uncharted 3: Drake's Deception Gameplay Reveal," PlayStation Blog, December 17, 2010.

term used to describe difficult job conditions, such as long hours, no weekends off, no vacations, or being given too little time to complete tasks.[205] It was the first time in Naughty Dog's history to split up the studio into two teams to work on developing two separate games: Uncharted 3 and *The Last of Us.*

"What I remember most about all the projects is how we crunched, and it got worse with every project," Hennig explained. This time, it was different from before. "It was odd being on *Uncharted* and not being on *The Last of Us* and being able to objectively watch people crunching and seeing the effect it was having."[206] Now, she was better able to see the harmful effects of "crunch" on her coworkers from afar.

This crunch, combined with "creative differences," as Hennig called it, led to her decision to leave Naughty Dog in 2014.[207] "That cemented some of my desire [where I thought] if I ever get a chance, if I was ever to have a studio, I'd do it differently," she said about her time at the company.[208]

She followed her position at Naughty Dog up with working as senior creative director at Electronic Arts (EA). There, she again worked as the lead writer for the Visceral Games' *Star Wars* project—or Ragtag, as the project was covertly called, to

205 Dean Takahashi, "Amy Hennig Interview."

206 Ibid.

207 Ibid; "Uncharted PS4 Writer Amy Hennig Leaves Naughty Dog," IGN Entertainment, June 24, 2020.

208 Jason Schreier, "The Collapse of Visceral's Ambitious Star Wars Game," Kotaku, G/O Media, October 27, 2017.

help keep their project a secret.[209] Visceral Games had been working on the *Star Wars* game since 2013, and they wanted the game to be a "story-based, linear adventure" in the style of *Uncharted* games.[210]

Unfortunately for Hennig, the same issues from Naughty Dog followed her: long work hours, issues with management, and high turnover rates. The studio was bleeding staff, and recruiters from other companies commented on the steady stream of former Visceral employees looking for other opportunities.[211] Still, she persevered.

That was, until EA decided to kill the *Star Wars*-themed game in October 2017 and shut down Visceral Games studios entirely. Why? "In its current form, it was shaping up to be a story-based, linear adventure game...We have been testing the game concept with players...It has become clear that to deliver an experience that players will want to come back to and enjoy for a long time to come, we needed to pivot the design," said EA's statement.[212]

Most of this news had been kept secret from the public, so it was to the surprise of the public that Hennig announced quitting her position at EA in January 2018. "I'm not doing anything *Star Wars*," Hennig told Eurogamer. "And, who

---

209 Ibid.

210 Dave Tach, "Visceral's Star Wars Game is 'In the Style of Uncharted,'
     Nolan North Says," Polygon, Vox Media, June 29, 2015.

211 Jason Schreier, "The Collapse of."

212 Ibid.

knows what the future may hold, but that project is on the shelf now."[213]

Around the same time, Hennig spoke about the state of the "story-based" games that had made up so much of her career. "As much as people protest and say, 'Why are you cancelling a linear, story-based game? This is the kind of game we want,' people aren't necessarily buying them. They're watching somebody else play them online," Hennig said.[214]

The phenomenon of moving away from story-based games means that the production expenditure often outweighs the revenue, generally leaving the video game studio to look for other ways to support the costs of production. With that, another trend has emerged: non-traditional game monetization practices (meaning revenue made aside from the initial price of buying the game). However, these practices happen to upset many in the target demographic. Some examples of game monetization deemed unfair by many players include:

- DLCs ("Downloadable Content"), or extra paid-for content that add to a game's story or gameplay
- Loot boxes, a randomly received consumable virtual item, like clothing or weapons, that function similarly to gambling
- Subscription-based services, like pay-per-month services

213 Tom Phillips, "Uncharted Creator Amy Hennig Has Departed EA, and Her Star Wars Game Is 'on the Shelf'," Eurogamer, June 28, 2018.

214 Sammy Barker, "People Ask for Story-Based Games, but Don't Necessarily Buy Them," Push Square, January 22, 2018.

Such services can either be for good or for bad. Take, for example, the *Elder Scrolls V: Skyrim* (2011) series—an open-world fantasy survival game about exploring a world filled with magic and dragons. The development team added a DLC to the game titled *Dragonborn* (2013) that practically doubled the size of the world with plenty more content to explore. *Dragonborn* cost less than half of the original game at $19.99 compared to $49.99. This DLC is highly respected by *Skyrim* fans and caused them to respect the development company Bethesda even more.

Another example to demonstrate the opposite effect is *Star Wars Battlefront 2* (2017), an action shooter game set in the *Star Wars* universe released by EA. While the game received generally favorable reviews for its gameplay, its most damning flaw was the development team's decision to include micro-transactions in exchange for boosts in the game that would aid the player. For example, to play as Darth Vader, players would need to pay—unless the player wanted to grind through half a hundred hours of boring gameplay to unlock him.

For an $80 deluxe version of the game, this was simply unacceptable. An EA representative's diplomatic response to an infuriated post on Reddit denouncing the game's pay-to-play system has the most downvotes of all time across the entire site, with 667 thousand downvotes—beating out the previous "top downvoted post" champion that had twenty-three thousand downvotes.[215]

---

215 MBMMaverick, "Seriously? I Paid $80 To Have Vader Locked?," Reddit Post, accessed September 17, 2020; Mike Minotti, "EA's Defense of Star Wars: Battlefront II is Now Reddit's Most Downvoted Comment," VentureBeat, November 12, 2017.

While monetization has received negative press, Hennig notes that, oftentimes, this is the only way developers and publishers can make money, because development budgets keep increasing by the millions while consumer demand for one-off games simply doesn't sell enough.

After a brief stint as a writer and independent consultant for companies in 2018 through 2019, Hennig announced in late 2019 that she was starting up an indie gaming company involved in VR called Skydance Media. This new project is described as being "designed to reach gamers and non-gamers alike on emerging streaming platforms, new story-focused experiences…will employ state-of-the-art computer graphics to provide the visual[s] of [film], but with an active… experience that puts the audience in the driver's seat."[216] It seems that Hennig is taking her experiences and focusing on the player experience, not necessarily a game with the best graphics or cool new features.

Aside from Hennig's many accomplishments as a talented storywriter on game development projects, many have noted her being a woman in a male-majority industry. Many news outlets have pressed this issue with Hennig, but she has denied that sexism in the video game industry ever personally affected her. In fact, she has said, "Usually it has been men who gave me the opportunities I have had…I think this

---

216 Michael McWhertor, "Amy Hennig's New Studio Will Make 'Story-Focused' Games for 'Emerging Streaming Platforms'," Polygon, November 18, 2019.

is a young enough and progressive industry that there just isn't any of that." [217]

All in all, Hennig says she hasn't faced any problems being a woman in the video game industry. However, she does say that being a woman provided some perspective and reality to some issues. For example, on *Uncharted 2*, which features two prominent female characters in 3-D, Hennig recalls that she would suggest to the modelers, "Let's take it down. How about a C [cup]?" [218]

In Hennig's eyes, the game industry is a much of a meritocracy as an industry can be. She advises young people: "Put yourself in a position where lightning can strike." [219] If you put in the effort and show that you're dedicated, the industry will give you opportunities. If not, you probably won't last long—or get in at all.

---

217 "Ben Fritz, "How I Made It."

218 Ibid.

219 Ibid.

CHAPTER 10

TO NURTURE

"'The industry' isn't a single monolithic entity, and this becomes really clear when asking how we balance business and creativity. At the AAA level, business concerns have to come first: we've got to keep the lights on and the rent paid at the studio or else everyone's out of a job, so you make every compromise you need to in order to make sure that your games make enough money that you don't have to close the studio, and creativity is one of those things that you have to make the business case for or else it doesn't get in the game."

—IAN SCHREIBER

When I was around ages five to ten, aspiring to learn "game development" was something that would've earned scoffs from friends, teachers, and parents. This is something you can go back and find evidence of through search indexing:

take, for example, the website "Animation Arena." In 2005, they had a page with a list dedicated to "colleges and universities with programs that would help someone in their pursuit of a career in technical direction, character animation and video game design."[220]

However, of the twenty-five institutions they listed (ranging from the Savannah College of Art and Design to the Westwood College of Technology), only six had programs dedicated to "game"-anything. The rest were web design, flash design, 3-D modeling, motion graphics; all somewhat related to game development, but not curated for the game development process.

Many of the game developers who I've previously mentioned either self-taught a significant portion of the skills they needed to do their work today or learned fundamentals such as art or programming at college. The reason for this is because until recently, much of academia refused to view it as a "real" skill that could be taught in a classroom or lecture hall.

While I don't deny that you may have been able to receive quality secondary education in 2005 and use those exact skills in the workplace, it is difficult to argue that you could have gone into college gung-ho about game development and come out of it with applicable skills.

---

220 "Video Game Design School," Animation Arena, accessed August 25, 2020, distributed by The Internet Archive Wayback Machine.

However, things have changed. Game development is now the "hot" degree among many American colleges, ranging from the University of Southern California to Carnegie Mellon University.[221] Schools that offer free online courses like Harvard and Massachusetts Institute of Technology offer game development courses. Online schools like Udemy offer incredibly low-cost game development courses at $124.99 a pop, which are often marked down 50 percent off or more during site-wide sales.[222]

And when we go back and look at "Animation Arena" in mid-2020, on that same page I previously mentioned, there are now four separate categories ("Game Art Degree," "Digital Entertainment and Game Design," "Video Game Design and Programming," and "Video Game Design and 3-D Animation") dedicated to sharing information about game development-related secondary degrees, each with tens of schools listed.[223]

I was able to speak to Ian Schreiber, professor of game development at the Rochester Institute of Technology, about what led him to becoming a game development professor in that climate. RIT is ranked among the top schools to receive a degree in game design as of 2019, coming out at eighth place

---

221 Jacob Akins, "Video Game Design Colleges | 77 Best Schools for 2020," Successful Student, May 29, 2020.

222 Christina Williams, "Udemy Discounts Courses Up To 95% Off For Flash Sale," *New York Post*, March 30, 2020.

223 "Video Game Design School," Animation Arena, accessed August 25, 2020.

on the Annual Princeton Review list.[224] The Review studies quality of school programs and future career placement.

Initially, Schreiber started off with a programming focus. "My parents told me that if I wanted to make video games, I'd better learn to program...so I did," he explained to me. He graduated from Carnegie Mellon University with a BS in mathematics and computer science that same year. He bounced around several companies, first starting out as a programmer for an information systems company, then moving on to game programming in 2000.

"I had considered a teaching career even back when I was in college," he explained, "so it wasn't surprising to anyone who knew me that I ended up going that route." Schreiber was always the kid who helped peer-tutor their friends when he was younger. That translated into mentoring local schools during his early times in the industry. He found that he greatly enjoyed the process of teaching others concepts to help them understand what he already did.

The catalyst for his becoming a teacher of game development happened in 2006, after he suffered a second mass layoff from his position as a game developer after three years in the position. It was his wife's turn to decide where to move again, particularly because of her own struggles with encountering a glass ceiling as a scientist with a BS degree; she needed to return to grad school if she wanted to advance in her career.

---

224 Ellen Rosen, "RIT video game design programs again ranked among the best," Rochester Institute of Technology, March 12, 2019.

After applying to several programs, his wife found a program she wanted to pursue in Columbus, Ohio. And as Schreiber remarked, "Columbus in 2006...[was] not exactly a hotbed of game development." So, to Schreiber, it looked like his hopes for a teaching career in game development might fizzle out.

Yet, it was through total coincidence that around the same time, a company that Schreiber was contracted for had him visit Ohio University in Athens, Ohio (an hour and a half drive out of Columbus), to discuss with students and faculty about a potential research grant application—for the company, of course.

Schreiber made a visit to Ohio. Again, by pure coincidence, once Schreiber had finished his discussion, one faculty member pulled him aside and told him they were looking for someone to teach game development—did he know anybody? "And I said, 'Yes, me!'" Schreiber answered. So he started working at Ohio University, moving to Ohio so he and his wife could work in their respective careers. His position there lasted just a year, but it convinced him that he could do this—that he could teach game development in a university setting.

Schreiber continued to teach game development through the Columbus State Community College as an adjunct professor, teaching game art, animation, and programming. He also started up a position as an online instructor of game development in 2009: every summer from 2009 through 2011, he taught subjects like game design concepts, game balance, and non-digital game design. And he's left those web pages up for anybody to view for free, though they must purchase his physically published textbook separately (yes, *his*; more on that, later).

Later, Schreiber decided to pursue a master's in game development. After applying to many programs, he was accepted to the prestigious Savannah College of Art and Design (SCAD) for interactive design and game development in 2008. Luckily, he'd be able to pursue that degree online *whilst* being an adjunct professor at SCAD.

During his time at SCAD, he also managed to publish his first textbook on game design, *Challenges for Game Designers,* with his colleague and fellow game designer who has worked on games like *Wizardry 8* (2001) and *Dungeons & Dragons: Heroes* (2003), Brenda Brathwaite. They jumped into writing the textbook with the mentality of, "We already know everything that would go into this book so this [will] be the easiest thing ever," to finding out it actually wasn't as easy as he'd thought. Still, he pushed through to the end. Now, this book is one of many popular game design textbooks out there—even I used the textbook for my course on game development.

After earning his degree at SCAD, Schreiber worked remotely as a game designer for Loot Drop from March 2011 to May 2012.

When I asked him about the briefness of his many positions, he responded with laughter. "Games are always on the cutting edge of tech, one of the handful of industries that tends to push current hardware to its limits and drives innovation on the new hardware," he described. "This is not the place to go where you can cling to the ways you were taught in college and keep doing the same thing you've always done, not if you want to succeed."

During that time, he managed to publish a second book, *Breaking Into the Game Industry: Advice for a Successful Career from Those Who Have Done It,* again co-written with Brenda Brathwaite. This time, the book covered practical advice such as how to network in the game industry and what should be in the portfolio of a game developer. It's a funny and realistic guide that I'd highly recommend if you're interested in building a career in the industry.

FUN FACTS:
Classes he teaches: Game Design & Development I, Game Balance, Gameplay and Prototyping
Favorite Games: *Final Fantasy VI* (1996), *Dungeons and Dragons*
Game he'd create with infinite resources: *"I wouldn't make a single game; instead I'd build an experimental gameplay lab, hire an army of students, and have them doing game-jam-like prototypes on a continual basis, studying what kinds of constraints seem to lead to the most creative outputs, and then taking those prototypes that show the most promise and transferring them to a small team that can build it out into a full moderate-sized experience. So, basically, with infinite time and resources I'd do exactly what I'm doing now, just at a larger scale."*

Luckily, in 2014, Schreiber managed to land a position at RIT as a part-time professor and research faculty member at the growing game development program (and later in 2017 as an assistant professor). His position included research on the game development process, including trying to answer questions, like: How can we make programming enemy AI more efficient? What kind of crazy, wacky idea can we represent in this game engine? And so on. "I do a lot of experimental work myself that is literally 0 percent sellable and 100 percent creativity, and my position as research faculty lets me get away with that," Schreiber remarked.

This would later become a full-tenure track position. With a secure standing, he now had the ability to devote his life to teaching game development to young adults.

Through teaching, he's had many rewarding moments. Among the examples he listed was seeing his students get hired by their dream game companies or launch their careers. Another example was having his students show up to class excited about the material as much as he is. "Being able to answer questions that seem basic to me but are life-altering insights to the students who haven't been there [is so rewarding]," he elaborated.

Still, there have been crunch periods. Because he balances academia with professional game development, he encounters different types of frustrations, though most of it boils down to long working hours and facing repetitive, demanding work. On the industry end, "it feels bad when it's mandated from above—[it] feels unfair that I should have to be breaking my neck because of someone else's poor planning," Schreiber lamented.

As for academia, because teaching is more self-directed, it feels bad because it's self-inflicted damage, whether due to poor planning or taking on too many tasks than he should've. "I have no one to blame but my own self."

Schreiber's also been featured in games news sites like *Kotaku*, discussing his thoughts on the consequences of this very topic in the game development industry, thanks to his large following he's built up through his time in the game development industry. Take for example an article entitled, "How Game Companies Use Credits To Reward, Or Punish Developers" from *Kotaku* in January 2020. This article covered the lack of standards for who gets put in the credits for a video game (that work similarly to credits at the end of a movie)—allowing for the possibility of people who worked on a game not being listed due to bad relations with the company, as an example.

"Having accurate, verifiable credits isn't part of the certification process for Apple or Steam or Nintendo or anywhere else," Schreiber wrote in an email to *Kotaku*, "So studios are more or less free to do whatever they want, with no consequences if they choose to ignore the standard."[225]

Schreiber doesn't work in game development because of pursuit of material reward or status. It's a labor of love. "Games were always a huge part of my identity," he said, and he's played games all his life, starting on an *Atari VCS*, a video game console from 1977, when he was six, and still plays

---

225 Forest Lassman, "How Game Companies Use Credits to Reward, or Punish, Developers," Kotaku, January 9, 2020.

games to this day. He has kids of his own now, too, so getting to see their reactions to both modern and classic games is special to him because they hold nostalgic value for him as well.

As a professor of game design and a professional game designer himself, he has succeeded in a field that was relatively unknown a decade ago. The perseverance and dedication he held to his craft is what has gotten him to where he is today. Writing textbooks and a blog on the subject, being interviewed by press, and actively partaking in research have all helped him solidify his position in the industry.

CHAPTER 11

OPTIMIZATION OBSESSED

"Games are very difficult to engineer for because you can't tell if something is fun until you've built enough of it to play it. So, the designs in games radically changed sometimes week to week, and that changes the software. Then the business side is crazy as well, funding comes funding goes, but the technology side is my favorite, and I love it when they change things [up]."

—LARRY MELLON

Being an obsessive learning junkie is generally something that sounds better in theory than in practice. Balancing heavy workloads during the daytime with learning new software or skills at night tends to be a draining, demanding exercise that most cannot keep up with. One must be both motivated and passionate to accomplish such a task. Larry Mellon, though, is one of those few that can do just these things—in the gaming industry, no less.

Larry Mellon is a systems optimization expert. He loves to find inefficiencies in systems and make them efficient. Take, for example, the way your bookcase is organized in your office. He'd love to sort them from red to blue, alphabetically, and based on book height, just to see which would be the most efficient method of finding the book you needed. Or better yet, synthesize the shortest line of code to have a computer do that work for him. He has taken that passion—programming efficiency—and applied it to his life with bold ambition.

Mentoring, start-ups, private industry, and military sector work are all ways he has applied this approach to his professional life. In each of these situations, he has best applied his skills by working on computers. The best way to explain what he does, or "in English," as Larry likes to say, is that he's essentially taking any part of the engineering or programming for a computer system, such as within an MMO game structure, and improve how it functions. For example, this might mean making sure that assets that are not visible to the player's screen do not take up graphical processing power for the player's computer during gameplay. Or it could be making sure that communications between two computers are optimized, reducing lag between the host and the third party.

"I'm not happy unless I'm obsessing about something complicated," Larry said to me at the start of our interview. "I was pretty poor growing up, but my mother managed to find money once a month for me to go to the used bookstore with a paper grocery bag, and I was allowed to fill it up with whatever I wanted to read," he told me as an example of his obsession with efficiency since he was young. "When you're optimizing for space and a bag, you actually have to consider book dimensions." That was just one example of many of his obsessions; and of course, this has translated to his career and interests as he has grown older.

He got his first chance at playing video games on the school computers in college with friends. There, he studied computer programming. He got into research by the time he was in grad school at the University of Calgary, purely working on improving the computer processes for research scientists involved in networking, healthcare, and chip design. He'd performed what is called "paralleled simulation:" taking their problem and breaking it apart for multi-threaded execution, then running it on the supercomputers at the labs at his school. His entire job revolved around optimizing computer systems to work as efficiently as possible

During this time, he also got into customer-facing roles. When the marketing department from a company met him, they said: "'Wow, a technical guy who also speaks English! This is awesome!'" and "[they] kidnapped me," Mellon said while laughing. He's someone who not only wants to do his work, but he also wants to be able to tell others what he's doing, too, to make the communication also as efficient as possible.

By the time he'd earned his master's, he was "hot shit"—his words, not mine. "We were hotshots coming out of grad school to do a start-up in parallel computing," he explained, "[but] our software base ended up Frankenstein-ing. We lost control of schedules, features…we were mainlining towards death. So we bought a bunch of books on scaling the software development process, and that really hooked me." Ever since then, he's become obsessed with the software development process—and making it run well.

Eventually, the start-up was acquired by the Science Applications International Corporation (SAIC) in the early 1990s, one of the largest technology contractors for the United States government that still operates to this day. So, Mellon began working in programming MMO simulators for the military. His work involved creating simulations that allowed cadets to practice what being in war was like, before going into the actual war.

FUN FACTS:
Games He's Worked On: *The Sims 2* (2005)
Companies Worked: EA, SAIC, KIXEYE, HumaNature Studios
Game he would like to create: A new type of MMO that has efficient infrastructure that pieces together new slices of the world when you need them. A real-time strategy RPG with believable characters. A team of do-gooders travels back in time with modern medicine and technology to get the New World prepared for the European invasion in the 1400's.
Favorite Game: *Risk* (1957-), *Factorio* (2020), *Civilization VI* (2016)

The stint at SAIC lasted for seven years until Mellon felt tired of working on similar problems repeatedly. He was under-stimulated at work and needed something new to challenge him. His wife came to him one day and she said, "All right, I'm tired of you stomping around the house late at night grumbling to yourself. I'm willing to put up with you stomping around the house talking excitedly to yourself. So find something that's equally as complicated but with a better class of person." Mellon took that advice; within a year, by 2001, he had made the career shift to work in systems optimization for games.

Mellon transitioned to work for the Maxis Studio with Electronic Arts (EA) as the publisher on *The Sims Online* (2002) to program large-scale multiplayer functionality for the games (the same project that Gordon Walton worked on). Mellon began to find a love for the complexity of game programming. "Games are very difficult to engineer for because you can't tell if something is fun, until you've built enough of it to play it," he explained. "How do I take [the current game software] I have now, and move it into that direction?"

Unfortunately, *The Sims Online* would go on to become a financial and project disaster. "Why it failed commercially is EA at the time was run by marketing idiots," Mellon said. "Their special power was dominating the marketing of games, [and] they saw the game as almost secondary to that." The game also asked players for a subscription fee of $9.99 a month—quite a high price for the time.

"So we told them flat out, look, to hit the schedule you wanted, we had to cut two thirds of the game features," Mellon recalled, saying that they had only finished the multiplayer framework for the game a month prior to going live. And that excluded months of testing and smoothing out that would need to happen for the game to work as a fun, successful multiplayer game. Otherwise the game would be bogged down with server-side errors that would display as "You could not connect to the server. Try again?" errors, frustrating players to no end.

They could launch it when management wanted to, but the game would be "thin," and the numbers unsatisfactory, to say the least. Mellon and his team of engineers offered suggestions of an improved timeline, and to that, EA management replied: "This is senior VP worldwide, we're prepared to ship shit in a box, because...*Sims* fans will buy anything. So ship the goddamn thing."

The game bombed. Andrew Park from *GameSpot* wrote in his review, "You'll frequently walk into a richly furnished house and find that instead of throwing a lavish party, all the players in the house are frantically playing chess to improve their logic skill."[226] EA wasn't happy with the sales numbers, and many dreary years later, they shut down the servers in 2008, after a brief re-branding of the game as *EA-Land*.[227]

After his time at EA, Mellon has worked at several gaming companies—KIXEYE, Goodgame, Chimera—all the while still working in systems optimization. In February 2019, he

---

226 Andrew Park, "The Sims Online Review," GameSpot, December 18, 2002.

227 Daniel Terdiman, "'EA Land' Closing Just Weeks after Debut," *CNet*, April 29, 2008, distributed by The Internet Archive Wayback Machine.

took up a job at HumaNature Studios as a technical director to work in an indie start-up environment. The project is funded by Google (cough—$20 million for solely the art pipeline isn't nothing) and is an attempt to find a unique game that could get more players for Stadia, Google's new online streaming-slash-console service. Because the studio is located in Maui, Hawaii, it fulfilled Mellon and his wife's dreams of living on a tropical island. Add to that the fact that one of Mellon's dreams has been to start up a distributed University for the Pacific Islands, and you can see why he moved over in a jiffy.

Unfortunately, the funding for HumaNature dwindled, and Mellon began thinking of switching careers once more. "I've been in games for about twenty years now, and it's time to look for a change," he said to me, though he isn't exactly sure in which direction to head. If he's looking for something even more complicated than system and programming optimization for games, though, he just might be out of luck.

During his times of working with different companies, Mellon has been a leader, and he hasn't been afraid to stand up to oppressive management. He shared with me another example of how he dealt with disorganization in the workplace.

Mellon had just figured out an inefficiency in the architecture of the programs they were using. He'd just joined the company a year and a half into launch; could he really ask his bosses and coworkers to throw out their *entire* architecture and create a new one?

"When I first brought it up, people turned white. It was the biggest technical risk in the project, and the thought of changing it scared them shitless," he joked. "It meant they just spent a year and a half building the wrong thing."

So, he dialed up the pressure on his colleagues. He started by writing a "white paper:" an authoritative report that informs the reader about a complex issue to help the reader solve it. He wrote up what the costs would be of changing the architecture, what would be the ramifications of not switching, and why they should make the switch. Then, he took that white paper to every single senior engineer in the company except the two who were opposed to the idea and got them to read it over and revise it with their own expertise.

Mellon then took the white paper to the executive team, and they did what he expected: each executive turned to their favorite engineers, the ones he'd talked the white paper over with, and asked them what they thought. "They all knew the right answer, because I had used them to help build the white paper," Mellon explained. "It was an incredibly contentious decision that people didn't want to make at all or were afraid of, [that] I managed to pull off in a day and a half by working at the grassroots level." He's applied that attitude toward every single one of his projects since.

Aside from his boldness in approaching leaders to fix inefficiencies, Mellon is also a dedicated mentor. "I totally groove on it," he exclaimed. "Just watching the little lights come on in their eyes and seeing them start to do things is awesome." He recalls a time he was mentoring employees and he heard that they started doing peer reviews of each other's work.

When Mellon asked why, they answered: "So that our stuff has a higher chance of passing when it gets to you." "Like, awesome!" Mellon said in an encouraging tone I could tell he reserved for students who excelled.

What we can learn from Mellon's experiences is that obsession with a topic is certainly a good indicator of what direction to head in. It's also that pursuing what you want, sometimes aggressively, is necessary in the game industry. He posts on LinkedIn about what jobs he wants (mentoring and hands-on coding) and where he wants to work (internationally). It's also about being kind, too; he takes great joy in mentoring those less experienced in himself, but not in a way that sugarcoats criticism. In the end, it all really comes down to being bold in your pursuit of what you love.

PART 3

INDEPENDENT GAME DEVELOPMENT

CHAPTER 12

WORKING UNDER THE MOON

"I think it makes sense that I worked entirely alone...I wanted to do all the music, the art."[228]

—ERIC BARONE

Now that we have covered both leadership and employment in the gaming industry, I would like to move to independent game development (or "indie gaming") in this section.

Independent game development refers to companies wherein little to no financial, technical, or marketing support is received from a large game publisher. So far, the development companies of those we have looked at were always affiliated with a publisher (save for Walton with *Crowfall* and Urquhart with *Pillars of Eternity*). Working with a publisher often

---

228 Sam White, "Valley Forged: How One Man Made the Indie Video Game Sensation Stardew Valley," *GQ Magazine*, March 20, 2018.

requires working under strict deadlines and expectations of the publisher, as were mentioned in the chapters of Cage and Miyazaki—strict deadlines and expectations that some developers do not care for.

By choosing not to work with a publisher, developers forsake the financial stability they could be receiving. It is certainly riskier. However, they are allowed significantly more temporal and creative freedom; after all, no one is telling them what to make. Yet since no one is telling them what to make, no one is paying them, either. Payday only comes if you manage to hit it big with a successful marketing campaign or by coincidence—if the online masses leap on your game, for whatever reason.

I'd now like to delve into the first example of an indie game developer (or at least, right until the very end). *Stardew Valley*, released in 2016, gives players the experience of backcountry, small-town living—ironically, through a video game. It's a life simulator game with romance, puzzles, and lovable characters. The game was created by a single man: Eric Barone, who previously had no professional game development experience aside from small personal projects and a bachelor's degree in computer science. This incredible feat of perseverance and tact that has gotten Barone to where he is.

Barone grew up in Seattle, Washington, in a rural area outside of the city. He started playing games just as most kids did in the late '80s and early '90s: on the Super Nintendo system, playing games like *Final Fantasy* (1987-) and *Chrono Trigger* (1995-). One of his favorite games, though, was *Harvest Moon* (1996-): a simple farm simulation game in which the player collects materials and trades them for money to expand their farm. It isn't too aggressively capitalistic, either—the game instead puts players at peace with its mild-mannered characters and story. And that was Barone's favorite part about it.

Barone wanted to work in the game industry in spite of understanding its volatility. He got a degree in computer science at University of Washington Tacoma, graduating with a BS in 2011. With his degree, he tried to apply for multiple jobs, but was rejected countless times.

He was living with his girlfriend Amber at the time and of course wanted to have a "better" life—a bigger house, kids, marriage, financial stability—but he wasn't succeeding. He became hopeless in his job search. "I was just kind of nervous and awkward...I didn't do well at the interviews," Barone told Jason Schreier in *Blood, Sweat and Pixels*, a book covering the stories of game developers.[229]

Barone realized he needed to be more practical with his job goals and add something to his resumé. And so he got to work, teaching himself coding, building a small project that would soon become the foundation for the now-famed *Stardew Valley*. It started out as a fan-made alternative to the *Harvest Moon* series. "I didn't really have any sort of deliberate plan or anything...I just had my intuition as to

---

229 Jason Schreier, *Blood, Sweat, and Pixels: The Triumphant and Turbulent Stories Behind How Video Games are Made*, (New York City: Harper Paperbacks, 2017), 63.

what was the next important thing I should work on," Barone explained about his process.[230]

He found rather early into development that he wanted to increase the scope of the project. "My ambitions for the game grew over time," he explained. Barone originally wanted to post the game to Xbox Live Indie Games, a section of Microsoft's Xbox platform that allows any independent game developer to sell their games easily. However, he found that as he went along in development, he wanted the game to keep growing and growing.[231]

Stardew Valley is similar to *Harvest Moon* in many regards. It was inspired by the latter, after all. They're both calming farming simulators. Both have other characters with deep backstories. Both have trading and seasons.

FUN FACTS:
Games he's created: *Stardew Valley* (2016)
Companies Worked: Self-Employed
Favorite game: *Harvest Moon* (1996-)

To develop the game entirely by himself, he had to handle every aspect of the game, including programming, art, and design. Barone started by fleshing out the central area that the player would exist in: the farm. He then added farming

---

230 Sam White, "Valley Forged."

231 Tom Marks, "Interview: What's Next for Stardew Valley," PC Gamer, Future US Inc., March 10, 2016.

mechanics like crops and livestock. He later tossed in the other villager characters, a combat system, and a cave area. The artwork for the characters' portraits were redone about ten times. [232] "I put in thousands of hours on pixel art just to get better at it and better at it," he says. "I just persevered and forced myself to learn. You realize the thing that you thought was good actually isn't...that's just an endless cycle."[233]

Still, Barone never considered asking others for help, let alone asking for a project teammate. "I think it makes sense that I worked entirely alone," he recalls. "I wanted to do all the music, the art."[234] Barone was working about ten to twelve hours a day every day of the week, essentially seventy- to eighty-four-hour work weeks, dedicated to *Stardew Valley*.[235]

A year into working on his game, he posted his project to Steam Greenlight in September 2012, another popular video game publishing service popular among large studios and independent developers alike. It was an easy way of getting word out early during development. He thought he'd have the game ready in a couple of months, and he declared as such on Steam. And it worked—soon enough, his game was starting to catch the attention of online gaming communities.

Posting *Stardew Valley* to Steam also caught the attention of Chucklefish, a publishing studio of indie video games.

232 Jason Schreier, *Blood, Sweat, and Pixels*, 63.

233 Sam White, "Valley Forged."

234 Ibid.

235 Chris Baker, "The 4 Years of Self-Imposed Crunch That Went into Stardew Valley." Gamasutra, March 9, 2016.

"Anyone [could] see the potential early on," Finn Brice, founder of Chucklefish said in an interview with Jason Schreier. The publishing studio decided to sign on Barone, with the deal of 10 percent of profits going to Chucklefish, and Barone receiving legal and marketing help from the company.[236]

What Barone initially assumed to be a couple more months of development soon became a couple more years. Barone let the creative work consume him, even letting his relationship with his girlfriend slip into the background. It was to the point where he dreaded seeing her parents and the questions about his career ambitions and his game.[237]

You might be wondering: what about finances? He's not making any money during the development of the game, right? You'd be correct. To support himself, he picked up an usher job at the Paramount Theater in Seattle for a couple nights a week to help pay the bills. His girlfriend Amber also picked up a job as a lab technician in 2015, and later became a graduate student who could offer a stipend as some pay.

It also didn't help that Barone didn't interact with anybody other than Amber. His usher job provided him some brief interaction with the outside world, but aside from that, he worked seventy-hour-plus workweeks alone in his apartment.[238] He kept up working out and went on walks, but he lived mostly in solitary confinement. However, that was a sacrifice he was willing to make.

---

236 Jason Schreier, *Blood, Sweat, and Pixels*, 65.

237 Jason Schreier, *Blood, Sweat, and Pixels*, 63.

238 Chris Baker, "The 4 Years."

Many times, Barone thought of giving up on *Stardew Valley*. The repetitive monotony of staring at the same characters, same dialogue, same artwork of a pixel art tree had worn down on him. As a solo developer, he lacked any reliable outside perspectives who could critique his game. Worst of all, he couldn't tell if his game was actually *fun*. "You lose all objectivity about your game. I had no idea when the game was fun. In fact, I thought it was garbage even up until a few days before release."[239]

Luckily, he had the backing of a publisher that would support him through these woes and provide an outside perspective. Chucklefish quietly signed on three Twitch streamers called Bexy, Siri, and Prens to playtest his game in private. They let him know of bug fixes, collectively playtesting around five hundred hours total that Barone could work on fixing.[240]

Chucklefish's support provided Barone with the outside perspective he desperately needed. As the release date came approaching, Chucklefish's PR department sent out free codes to play the game to Twitch streamers to give a sneak-peek into the *Harvest Moon*-like PC game. Barone was opposed to the idea at first: "I was afraid that people would see it on Twitch before launch and then they'd feel like they'd already seen the game and they weren't going to buy it," he said.[241] However, *Stardew Valley* appeared on Twitch's front page almost every day for the following week, foreshadowing high community interest in his game.

239 Jason Schreier, *Blood, Sweat, and Pixels*, 76.

240 Jason Schreier, *Blood, Sweat, and Pixels*, 65.

241 Jason Schreier, *Blood, Sweat, and Pixels*, 76.

On the night of February 25, 2016, just a couple of hours before he was expected to release the game to the public, Barone encountered a game-breaking bug. Yes, the kind that can truly ruin the entire gameplay experience: we're talking on the level of not being able to throw Pokéballs at Pokémon without the game crashing. It sent Barone into panic mode. He can't even recount what the bug was, now. All he remembers is pulling an all-nighter to fix it. "It was very stressful but also exhilarating," Barone recalled.[242]

On February 26, 2016, *Stardew Valley* was released to the public. In just two weeks, the game had sold over four hundred thousand copies, and over a million over the course of the next two months. As of early 2020, the game has sold more than ten million copies.[243] Considering that the game's price was $14.99, this essentially equates to $150 million in pure capital. Considering Chucklefish's 10 percent cut, that's a very rough estimate of $135 million in Barone's pocket.

Video games are often put under scrutiny for what platforms they choose to release to. In recent years there's been a conflict between "console" users, who primarily use Microsoft's Xbox platform or Sony's PlayStation platform, and PC users. Console users tend to prefer performance and innovation; PC users prefer that, as well as games that they can play for extended periods of time (which *Stardew Valley* just so happens to be). The game takes advantage of the PC platform, which makes up nearly a quarter of the video game market,

---

242 Sam White, "Valley Forged."

243 Andy Chalk, "Stardew Valley Has Sold More Than 10 Million Copies," *PC Gamer*, January 23, 2020.

or \$35.7 billion of total video game software sales in 2019.[244] Since then, *Stardew Valley* has been ported to PlayStation 4, iOS, and the Nintendo Switch, to name a few.

When it comes to Barone's "no strategy" strategy, instead relying on honesty and straightforwardness, we can see it reflected in the community that blossomed from *Stardew Valley*. At launch, pirates torrenting (sharing the game file for free without paying the creator) the game said they "felt bad" and decided to buy the game, en masse.[245]

Barone even met the creator of *Harvest Moon*, Yasuhiro Wada, in 2016. They sat down and played each other's games. When asked by PCGamer about having Wada play *Stardew Valley*, Barone replied: "Surreal, but really awesome."[246] He also made the achievement of making the "30 Under 30" of *Forbes'* Games list.[247]

But the money and success aren't a standalone thing for somebody like Barone, who worked on the game by himself. One misconception fans of video games may have is that once a video game is published, the developer rakes in the money and drops the project completely. That couldn't be farther

---

244 Tom Wijman. "The Global Games Market Will Generate \$152.1 Billion in 2019 as the U.S. Overtakes China as the Biggest Market," Newzoo, June 18, 2019.

245 Patricia Hernandez, "A Surprising Number of People Feel Bad for Pirating Stardew Valley," Kotaku, March 2, 2016.

246 *PC Gamer,* "The Creators of Stardew Valley and Harvest Moon Talk to Us about Farm Games," December 1, 2016, video, 16:58.

247 "Eric Barone," *Forbes,* accessed August 19, 2020.

from the truth. Barone himself still works on debugging and patching for *Stardew Valley* in 2020, and if anything, works even harder to fix the bug reports his fans submit. "Suddenly you feel as if you owe a lot of people a lot of things," Brice of Chucklefish described about how developers often feel about their fame. Barone would frequently pull all-nighters to fix the issues that arose.

The work on his game is far from done. One of the major tasks that all developers of game studios must do is continue to release bug fixes even after the game is released, especially now that this is becoming more and more convenient to do by way of automatic game updates on console systems. Starting on February 26, 2016, Barone was already working on bugs, day after day, for around fifteen hours a day.[248]

In spite of the overwhelming pressure, Barone continues to work on bug fixes as well as general game improvement patches to this day. Four years since the release of *Stardew Valley* for PC, on February 26, 2020, Barone posted to Twitter: "Now that 1.4 is out on all intended platforms, I'd like to announce that there will be another free content update (1.5)..it's currently in the works!"[249]

He doesn't do that as much anymore, but he still works away at *Stardew Valley* to this day. His Twitter feed is littered with descriptions of bugs he's trying to fix or has just fixed. November 26, 2019: "Okay, PSA everyone, right now sending just an emoji in game, with no text, will cause the game to

248 Chris Baker, "The 4 Years."

249 ConcernedApe, Twitter Post, November 26, 2020, 3:31 p.m.

crash."[250] December 20, 2018: "Also, want to let the Switch players know that we've got a patch on the way to address the frame rate issue (and the weird lighting bug)...doing everything possible to get that patch to you as soon as possible!"[251]

Barone made quite a few sacrifices to work on *Stardew Valley*, including a stable income, relationships, and career development. Luck was also involved in the fact that he had a girlfriend willing to support him, financially and relationally, throughout the experience. Certainly, no formula exists to what he did—I can't promise you that if you follow in his exact same steps, you'll get the same outcome.

Like many other developers, he made personal sacrifices. However, unlike most of them, he worked almost entirely by himself. They both built up loyal communities, but through different means: others with the help of a large publishing studio's name and backing, and Barone much by organic online interaction. While others were approached by large publishers, Barone was approached by a much smaller one.

Why I share Barone's story is so that you can understand the challenges faced by a lone developer and how they are different from a development company with many employees. There is the unknown of whether the game will make any money, or whether you will self-publish or a publisher will approach you. However, both situations often require devoting most of your time to the endeavor.

---

250 ConcernedApe, Twitter Post, November 26, 2019, 2:22 p.m.

251 ConcernedApe, Twitter Post, December 20, 2018, 3:37 p.m.

CHAPTER 13

FROM THE BLOCK, UP

"I make games because it's fun...but I don't make games with the intention of them becoming huge hits... I'm not an entrepreneur. I'm not a CEO. I'm a nerdy computer programmer who likes to have opinions on Twitter."[252]

—MARKUS PERSSON

If one game defines the 2010s, it's *Minecraft*. Released on May 17, 2009 by Mojang, an independent Swedish game development company, it is the single best-selling video game of all time, selling over two hundred million copies across all consoles and platforms by 2020.[253] It still rakes in over one hundred million players a month and it regularly headlines

---

252 Jose Pagliery, "Microsoft Buys Minecraft for $2.5 Billion," CNN Business, Cable News Network, September 15, 2014.

253 "Cumulative Number of Copies of Minecraft Sold Worldwide as of May 2020," Statista, Ströer, accessed September 15, 2020.

the "Popular" pages of online video and streaming platforms like YouTube and Twitch, even a decade after its release. In a day and age where games come out with sequels once a year with loaded new features and storylines, what exactly is it about Minecraft that makes it such a bestseller—and who is the mastermind behind it?

Minecraft is deceivingly simple. It's a video game about placing blocks to build a base (imagine Legos but only being able to use the same 2x2 square pieces), hunt monsters, and become stronger so you can acquire rarer or sturdier blocks to build with. Unlike what you might expect, it's built in 16-pixel squared resolution, meaning everything looks very pixelated. The game's overworld is a 3-D world that includes biomes like forests, tundras, and deserts. It was initially developed by a single man in the late 2000s, who eventually acquired a team for legal reasons and technical support, which was later bought by Microsoft in 2014.

The creator of the game is Markus Persson, born in 1979 in Stockholm, Sweden. His interest in video games started at the young age of seven on his father's Commodore 128, an 8-bit home computer.[254] He'd make simple text adventure games, where the user would have to input something like, "kill the ninja," to get to the next part of the game.

His parents divorced when he was twelve. Persson failed to finish high school, but his mother had him continue education by taking an online programming course, seeing

---

254 Alex Handy, "Interview: Markus 'Notch' Persson Talks Making Minecraft," Gamasutra, Informa PLC, March 23, 2010.

potential in his love for the craft.[255] By 2004, Persson got a job at Midasplayer, a video game company (later known as King. com, creator of *Candy Crush* [2012]) as a game programmer.

As Persson grew older, he started to spend time entering hobby programming contests unrelated to his job at Midasplayer: *Sonic Racer 4k* (2005), *Infinite Mario Bros* (2008), and *Left 4k Dead* (2009) were some of the games he made, just to name a few. These were all made for Java 4k programming competitions, in which a group of judges asked entrants to re-create popular video games in the Java language (a coding language in which, most of the time, the original games were not made).

As an example, here is a list of some of the basic contest rules from the 2006 Java 4K Programming Contest, a contest that Persson won with *Miners4k* (2006):

1. The final game package (byte code and resources) must be below or equal to 4096 bytes (equivalent to 4 kilobytes, or a page's worth of text in a word document)
2. Must be a playable game (cannot be a pointless animation)
3. Must be pure Java (no JNI)
4. Must be self-contained—no external resources (e.g. loading an animation from a website)[256]

---

255   Ryan Mac, "Inside The Post-Minecraft Life Of Billionaire Gamer God Markus Persson," *Forbes*, March 3, 2015.

256   "Java 4K Programming Contest." Java Unlimited, July 17, 2011, distributed by The Internet Archive Wayback Machine.

The competitions often handed out free copies of games, or game subscriptions, as prizes.

At Midasplayer, Persson befriended Jakob Porsér, a young developer who also liked making games outside of their day job. They worked on games together and uploaded them to online sites. Many of these games caught the eyes of players on indie Flash sites, and they soon gained a following.

Unfortunately, as most things go, their boss didn't like the fact that they were producing things outside of work. "We felt that we couldn't have someone working for us that at the same time was building his own gaming company," said Lars Markgren, Midasplayer cofounder who had hired Persson.[257]

In 2009, Persson left Midasplayer due to the conflict of interest. He started working at Jalbum, an online photo-sharing service that didn't care about him working on his own gaming hobbies.[258]

By May of that year, Persson had built *Minecraft*, a game about collecting trees and stone to use them to build things. It had a "survival mode," where players could die by getting hit by enemies, and a "creative mode," where players could use any blocks they wanted to construct buildings however they wanted without taking damage.

He posted it to TIGSource, an online indie gaming portal. Soon enough, a small community had formed: they saw

---

257   Ryan Mac, "Inside The Post-Minecraft Life."
258   Ibid.

potential, but players needed each other's' help just to figure out how to play the game. It was still rather rudimentary and came with no how-to manual, after all.

Persson started distributing an "alpha" version of *Minecraft* in 2009, selling for $13 a pop for an "in development" version. By March 2010, *Minecraft* had sold over six thousand copies of this "in development version" and had become very popular on 4chan, a rather notorious anonymous messaging board. *Minecraft* was also being offered for free at this time, too, on minecraft.net, though this version included limited gameplay features.

He quit his day job at Jalbum in June 2010 when *Minecraft* was selling four hundred copies a day.[259] He even got Porsér and his boss at Jalbum, Carl Manneh, to help him with the business. They called their new company "Mojang," which is "gadget" in Swedish.

His work ethic wasn't particularly complicated. "I'll still change my schedule a lot," Persson explained in a 2010 *Gamasutra* interview. "If I run into something tricky and interesting, I can stay up very late and try to get it working, but other than that I think my hours are mostly sane." He doesn't like drinking coffee at home, but he loves Red Bull.[260]

---

259 Ibid.

260 Alex Handy, "Interview."

FUN FACTS:

Games He's Worked on: *Wurm Online* (2006), *Minecraft* (2009)

Companies Worked: Midasplayer, Mojang

Favorite Games: *Doom* (1993-), *Monkey Island* (1990-), *Half-Life* (1998-)[261]

Persson also started to build an online presence. He often went by the alias of "Notch" whenever he posted online. He created a Twitter profile with a fedora-wearing icon, where he'd post uncensored, scathing opinions if he ever felt the need. Combined with his "indie" style of game development, which was extremely rare at the time, he became, in a way, an icon for gamers who had become tired of triple AAA gaming companies like Electronic Arts (the "cynical bastards," as Persson called them), who seemed to care more for profit than players. His followers liked his witty, sharp humor; how he cut to the chase instead of flowering his language. He was a fresh, wanted face in game development in the early 2010s.[262]

As *Minecraft* started to receive attention, Persson began receiving requests for interviews into just how and why he'd decided to make the game. *Minecraft* was unlike any game at the time: it didn't have guns or blood or a solid "You Win" screen at the end of it. All it had was low-resolution blocks,

---

261 Ibid.

262 Kevin Parrish, "Minecraft Creator Notch Says EA is Destroying Gaming," Tom's Hardware, Future US Inc., May 6, 2012.

and a procedurally generated world, meaning the computer created the worlds for the player, not the programmers.

"There's a certain elegance in telling the computer how to make a world to show to the player, rather than to tell the computer what world to show," Persson described.[263] Much of his Java 4K Programming challenges were similarly based on procedural generation, meaning the computer would use an algorithm to create data, as opposed to manual entry. It made it easier to fit worlds into the allotted 4 kilobytes, instead of trying to cram in pre-generated content.

Procedural generation is convenient because it saves storage on the computer and can make more with what is given. For example, procedural generation might create a level with rooms, ABBABABA, rooms "A" and "B" representing different types of rooms, randomly sorting the rooms into that order for the player to experience unpredictably. The next time the player opens up the software, the level might display the rooms as BABBABBB. However, if this were manually programmed, the programmer and level designer would have to work together to decide which room would go after which room *before* the player opened up the software to play the game. The entire concept works along the lines of the saying, "Give a man a fish, feed him for a day, teach a man to fish, feed him for life"—if fish were computer data.

Procedural generation can even do things like create art or music. It's essentially a basic form of artificial intelligence.

---

263 Alex Handy, "Interview."

Aside from the procedurally generated maps of *Minecraft*, its "open source" game development format was unique. The development of *Minecraft* was, and still is, fundamentally based on user feedback. *Minecraft* "Alpha" lasted from June 2010 to December 2010, "Beta" from December 2010 to November 2011, and now we're on the "Official" versions, released as 1.xx updates.[264]

"[Open source development] mostly helps me decide which of the infinite list of potential features to add first," Persson said about this method in March 2010. "I try to spend a lot of time on the official IRC ("Internet relay chat") channel for instant contact with the most hard core of the players. It eats up a lot of time, but I think it's worth it!"[265]

Because players could build whatever they wanted to in *Minecraft*, the potential was endless. Iconic buildings such as the Taj Mahal and the Tokyo Tower became famous builds during this time, often being posted on sites like YouTube for many tens of thousands of views.

In May 2012, Mojang released *Minecraft* for the Xbox 360 and sold more than one million copies in the first week. Mojang received deals for licensing agreements with clothing and publishing companies. *Minecraft*-branded apparel became a best seller at J!NX of San Diego, a gaming brand third-party clothing company. Egmont Publishing International sold

---

264 "Java Edition Version History," Minecraft Wiki, Gamepedia, Accessed August 20, 2020.

265 Alex Handy, "Interview."

over 7.5 million copies internationally when they published a book about *Minecraft*.[266]

Of the $150 million in gross profit in sales in 2012, Persson took gross profits of $101 million. After Mojang sold ten million copies of *Minecraft*, they took the whole staff to Monaco for three days of partying on yachts with plenty of expensive alcohol.[267]

Due to the successes of *Minecraft*, Persson gained god-like popularity within the game industry, receiving multiple awards such as the Game Developers Choice Award in 2011 for Best Debut Game and Best Downloadable Game, as well as the BAFTA (British Academy of Film and Television Arts) Game Award in 2012.

At first, Persson had tried to keep the company small. In a post excitedly titled, "Top ten movies of 2011!," dated December 31, 2011, Persson answered the question he'd received from many fans: Why doesn't Mojang hire more programmers for *Minecraft*? "One reason why *Minecraft* has managed to get as much personality as it does [is] that it's only been a couple of fairly nerdy game developers working on it."[268]

It was hard to keep that small-office feel, though, when *Minecraft* was expanding so much. By 2014, the game had been downloaded more than one hundred million times

---

266 Ryan Mac, "Inside The Post-Minecraft Life."

267 Ibid.

268 "Top Ten Movies of 2011!" The Word of Notch, Tumblr post, December 31, 2011.

and grossed well over $1 billion. It was hard to balance the programming-side with user feedback, especially when the fanbase was growing so rapidly.

In June of 2014, Mojang posted its End User License Agreement (EULA): a document stating that users could not profit off of *Minecraft*. On multiplayer servers, it had become common for users to exchange goods like high-level enchanted swords and diamond blocks for real-world money. The EULA prevented that.

This caused outrage among *Minecraft* players. This also meant a lot more bitter tweets being sent Persson's way.

"What I hadn't considered was that a lot more people cared about my games now...the pressure of suddenly having people care if the game got made or not started zapping the fun out of the project," Persson explained in the same Twitter post. "Turns out, what I love doing is making games. Not hyping games or trying to sell a lot of copies."[269]

It was around this time, too, that Persson started to feel disconnected from reality. Sure, he lived in the most expensive apartment of Stockholm, and he'd married his wife in the summer of 2011. But he decided to step down as head developer at Mojang to a less managerial role. His father had committed suicide after a long battle with substance abuse and depression in late 2011. And then Persson went through a divorce with his just-married wife in 2012, and he felt immense pressure to re-create another huge gaming

---

269 Ibid.

success. All of the pressures from his career and personal life became overwhelming.

He had another problem, too. People online just wouldn't leave him alone. "I was struggling with why [people are] so mean online," he told *Forbes* in an interview in 2015. "The mean comments...seem like they're written in a bigger font size almost." Combined with all of these pressures, he began to seek an exit to it all.[270] Unlike Barone, who strictly keeps his social media content related to his creative content, Persson regularly engaged in discussions with people online about sensitive political issues—which made the harassment and trolling worse.

Persson was tired of it. It was June 15, 2014, and he was sick with a cold at home. "Anyone want to buy my share of Mojang so I can move on with my life? Getting hate for trying to do the right thing is not my gig," he tweeted out of sheer impulse.[271]

Carl Manneh, then-CEO of Mojang, hadn't been notified Persson would share such a thing. He was at his house with his family when he read the tweet, and less than a minute later, a Microsoft executive was calling him. They wanted to know if Persson was serious. "I'm not sure—let me talk to him," said Manneh.[272]

---

270 Ryan Mac, "Inside The Post-Minecraft Life."

271 Ibid.

272 Ibid.

In the following week, Manneh spoke to countless executives at Microsoft, Electronic Arts, Activision Blizzard, and more. It was also during this time that Apple had bought Beats, the headphones manufacturer, for $3 billion, and Amazon bought Twitch for $970 million. Each electronics company was trying to gain footholds in different business territories that the others didn't have. Naturally, many large tech companies were interested in buying *Minecraft*, the up-and-coming game wildly popular with kids and young adults.

Ultimately, Manneh and Persson decided on Microsoft, who bought *Minecraft* for $2.5 billion on September 15, 2014.[273] The deal had just a few terms: Manneh, Porsér, and Persson would have their ties with the company and *Minecraft* completely severed. They also wanted none of their other forty-seven staff members at Mojang to be laid off when being acquired.[274]

It was a smart move for Microsoft. Plus, with Mojang being a Swedish company, Microsoft would receive a decent tax cut for the purchase.[275] Along with this deal came an official proclamation from Persson on Twitter: he was no longer going to work at Mojang, or on *Minecraft*.

"As soon as this deal is finalized, I will leave Mojang and go back to doing Ludum Dares and small web experiments," Persson said in an official proclamation. "If I ever accidentally

---

273 Jose Pagliery, "Microsoft Buys Minecraft."

274 Ryan Mac, "Inside The Post-Minecraft Life."

275 Jose Pagliery, "Microsft Buys Minecraft."

make something that seems to gain traction, I'll probably abandon it immediately."[276]

After the Microsoft deal, Persson purchased a $70 million home in Trousdale Estates, Beverly Hills of California—the highest sales price for a home in Beverly Hills at the time.[277] Despite the fact that he now had almost as much freedom in real life as he did in his games, Persson's thoughts on living in a mansion overlooking the Pacific Coast and Los Angeles quickly became dull, even miserable.

"Found a great girl, but she's afraid of me and my life style and went with a normal person instead," he posted to Twitter on August 29, 2015.[278] "Hanging out in ibiza with a bunch of friends and partying with famous people, able to do what I want, and I've never felt more isolated," from August 29, 2015.[279]

Nowadays, Persson scrolls through Reddit and Twitter whenever he feels like it. He ignores the trolls, often muting them. He still works on small gaming projects, but nothing significant. He sometimes goes out to nightclubs in Las Vegas, NV

---

276 Ian Paul, "Microsoft Buys Minecraft Maker Mojang for $2.5 Billion," PCWorld, IDG Communications, September 15, 2014.

277 Erin Carlyle, "'Minecraft' Billionaire Markus Persson Buys $70 Million Beverly Hills Contemporary with Car Lift," *Forbes*, December 18, 2014.

278 Notch, Twitter Post, August 29, 2015, 5:53a.m.

279 "Markus Persson: The Minecraft Billionaire Sending Lonely Late-Night Tweets from Ibiza," The Guardian, Guardian News & Media Limited, September 1, 2015.

and spends up to $180,000 a night. The group chat with him and his friends is titled "Farts."[280]

"I'm a little bit making up for lost time when I was just programming through my twenties," Persson commented about his habits. "When [I was] young [I] did not have a lot of money at all, so I thought, if I ever get rich I'm not going to become one of those boring rich people that doesn't spend money."[281]

Persson doesn't care if he's a one-hit wonder. He's far too rich for it to concern him. Now, he just makes games for fun—with plenty of boyish habits to boot.

Minecraft is probably one of those once-in-a-decade kind of wonders. What happened to him was an extremely rare combination of the right skills and the right idea at the same time. A game that allowed players to do whatever they'd like, regardless of graphics quality? People wanted that. An independently developed game by a small team with plenty of personality? People wanted that, too. That, combined with the popularity of the game on online forums and online services, allowed *Minecraft* to explode as a product.

You can't aim to have that happen to you, similarly to Eric Barone and *Stardew Valley*. It's really only a combination of luck and being at the right place at the right time. And despite Persson's glitzy lifestyle and indulgences in clubbing

280 Ryan Mac, "Inside The Post-Minecraft Life."

281 Ibid.

and real estate, we've seen that he, at times, feels lonely, and no longer like a "normal person."

So perhaps it's best that this is a rare occurrence. And this is by no means a discouragement for you to develop games by yourself—it would just be best to monitor your own mental health and know your own goals and limitations. And perhaps, like Barone, to limit your interactions with online fans to business only.

Still, I hope to not fear monger or dissuade with this information. Both Barone and Persson were aware of the large communities building up around their games during development. These loyal followings had already formed before they each officially released their games, when sales subsequently exploded. Neither of them went from zero to a million eyes on their project in a day.

You will also have an idea of how successful your game might be by the attention it receives pre-launch. Again, if you're comfortable with this and the financial and social implications of it, go for it. However, if you're not, take a step back and consider the aid of a publisher or external developers to offset the responsibility and fame.

CHAPTER 14

A ONE-MAN BAND

"When working alone on a game there's the constant unknown if the game is any fun, or if the idea even makes sense. [So it was a big deal] the first time I had other people play the prototype - seeing how much they enjoyed it."[282]

—JAN RIGERL

After learning about the extremes of Barone's and Persson's approach to independent game development, I'm sure that at this point you're hoping to never let your kid sign up for a game development course. Fear not: it is possible to be an independent developer without crazy amounts of fame or drama. In fact, it's possible to even lie low while still being successful.

Enter Jan Rigerl, a Swedish video game developer from Stockholm, Sweden, has taken quite a liking to slapstick comedy,

---

282 "Moving Out Monday #17 – DevM + SMG," Steam Community, May 4, 2020.

based on Italian improv plays from the sixteenth century, over his years as a game developer.

Rigerl started off wanting to do 3-D modeling and animation for special effects for film in the late '90s. He initially had little interest in working for the video game industry. While games had a large influence in his childhood, it was more for the sake of playing them rather than the possibility of making them.

He attempted to send his portfolio to target companies in the film industry, but he couldn't find any places that would take him. So instead, he sent out his portfolio to some video game companies, just for the hell of it. They liked Rigerl's work, and that was how he found his way in: as a 3-D modeler and animator for games.

Rigerl worked at gaming companies like Grin and King for a couple of years. However, he started to find the idea of working "under" somebody restrictive. And besides, he'd built up a group of friends who he could start a company with. "We just had more of a bigger need for programming than art at the time," he explained to me. That was how he started getting into the programming side of game development more seriously.

This would start Rigerl's love affair with independent game development. He worked with friends as a game developer at SQD Interactive from 2004 to 2006. Then he went to work for King.com, the same company that Markus Persson worked for around the same time, developing multiplayer flash games from 2006 to 2009—the longest form of "normal" employment he would have. He also dabbled in web development consulting for flash games through the late 2000s.

Flash games were popular then, though not so much now. Flash was a browser plugin produced by Adobe and integrated into the web browser for the user. By including Flash, the browser could do things like display animations and games, and even stream audio and video. However, it became outdated when HTML5, the newest version of the HTML language, came out in 2014.

FUN FACTS:

Games He's Worked On: *Moving Out* (2020), *Silly Sailing* (2017), *Extreme Forklifting* (2015)
Favorite Games: *Doom* (1993-), *Fallout 1* (1997) & 2 (1998), *X-Com* (1994)
Companies Worked: King, DEVM-Games
Game he'd create with infinite resources: Many smaller games than one large game; while he enjoys playing monster productions like *Cyberpunk 2077* (2020), it's not really something he'd like to work on.

Still, one thing irked Rigerl. It was not being able to work completely alone, having complete creative autonomy. On Rigerl's LinkedIn and website, he advertises himself as a "one-man band." Though I initially assumed it was due to a side interest in music (mostly because I simply couldn't believe that a single person could develop over twenty games by themself), it quickly became apparent from our conversation that it is because he prefers to work alone.

That was why Rigerl founded DEVM-Games in 2009 by himself, for himself. He worked in browser-based games, building projects with titles like *Monster Trucks 360* (2012), featuring isometric side-scroller monster trucks collecting coins, and *Surroubble* (2011), an updated take on the classic bubble shooter classic. Each of the projects would take around three months to complete.

Rigerl is also a diligent blogger. On his website, devmgames. com, aside from a log of all of the games he's worked on, he also keeps a development log where he writes about the process of programming and modeling. He's done this since the early days of working at DEVM-Games. He updates once every couple of months. Take this example from June 6, 2014:

Want bitmap fonts with an outline in Unity? Not as easy as it might seem since the built in feature for creating bitmap fonts packs the characters so tight that you can't add any shadow or outline. And no setting to add padding. So I made this little editor extension that makes it possible to import fonts created with tools like AngelCode Bitmap Font Generator or Glyph Designer. Anything that creates a .fnt-xml-file.[283]

Rigerl posted this to help other game developers get "bitmap fonts"—take any old regular font, like "Papyrus," and "bit"-ify it. Meaning, make the font look low-resolution, like the

---

283 "Unity Font Importer - Devlog," Dev-M Games, June 6, 2014.

text you'd find on the screen of an '80s arcade game. This tutorial helps developers convert any font they'd like into the "bitmap" version in the Unity game engine.

His other posts detail how his games are doing, from the developer and business side of things. For example, he described on May 29, 2013, about the conundrum for developing *Extreme Forklifting* for iOS and Android: "For my forklift project I don't think it's worth to invest [$4500 (USD)] to buy Unity Pro with iOS & Android support. I don't really expect to make much money from it. It's mostly just for fun and to learn some Unity."[284] Or from February 23, 2017: *"Desert Worms* was released in November, didn't do too well on iOS but has been getting quite a lot of users on Google Play. Closing in on six hundred thousand downloads now."[285]

These posts are a treasure trove of information for other game developers who want to find out exactly how the mind of a solo business owner and game developer works. "I wish I could buy the Pro version of this software, but I don't think it's worth it for $59/month" and "Trying to build the shaders in this engine is terrible for my GPU (Graphics Processing Unit). Thinking of purchasing an upgrade in a month or two so I can support 32GB RAM instead of 16GB," are just examples of the thoughts game developers may have (speaking of, that RTX 3080 processor sure looks nice...).

---

284 "LightmapLightApproximator.cs for Unity," Dev-M Games, May 29, 2013.

285 "Desert Worms," Dev-M Games, February 23, 2017.

Still, it's hard not to notice that Rigerl has been posting less and less since early 2016. And there's a reason for that: Rigerl was starting to work on a large game. A really large one; one that *just* might require the help of other people.

The game's title: *Moving Out*. Genre: physics-simulation, slapstick comedy. Concept: multiplayer-game where players toss furniture from a tenant's home to help them move out.

The idea for *Moving Out* came to Rigerl in mid-2016 when he was helping his friends move. He found that planning exactly how to move out furniture through doorways was similar to level designs in games. "What if moving houses was a game?" he asked. "Like a moving simulator?" his friend responded.[286] That was all the exchange needed.

Rigerl initially spent six months programming the game. This was a sign that something was going to be different about the project; he'd already doubled his usual game development time. To add to that, "I was feeling that the project was getting bigger," Rigerl explained. "[I thought] maybe it'd be best to partner up with someone else to help with it."

This feeling that the game was growing more than his previous titles came from his own intuition, rather than something like an online fanbase coming from Steam Greenlight or other Early Access platforms.

At that point in December 2016, *Moving Out* still lacked fitting 3-D assets for the "mover" characters, the items to be

---

286 "Moving Out Monday," Steam Community.

moved, and the appearance of the walls and overall house.[287] The movers were golden amorphous humanoid blobs that carried around boxes and a couch through gray-tiled walls.

Rigerl continued to work on the game through April 2017, when he eventually showed his prototype to SMG Studios, an Australian game development company. By then, Rigerl had incorporated a more streamlined stylistic look for his furniture assets, which he had more of (such as a sink, fridge, bathtub, couch, and cabinets). He even incorporated different types of character models, like a burger mover and a human mover. They could now move furniture through the house (which now looked more like an actual house with wallpaper and hardwood floors), which could leave scratches on the floors.

SMG Studios liked the game and wanted to work with him (although one criticism Dave Lockman had about the game was that characters couldn't jump).[288]

Rigerl had the chance to visit Melbourne, Australia, to see the development of the game. "It felt a little surreal at first," he recalled about seeing a large group of people playing something he'd developed. "When working alone on a game there's the constant unknown if the game is any fun, or if the idea even makes sense. [So it was a big deal] the first time I had other people play the prototype—seeing how much they enjoyed it."[289]

287 SMG Studio, Twitter post, April 30, 2020.

288 "Moving Out Monday," Steam Community.

289 Ibid.

The two parties continued to work together through early 2019. Initially, Rigerl and SMG agreed that SMG would publish the game, but after the release of their announce trailer, Team 17, a British video game company that has been around since 1990, contacted them with interest in supporting the game to help publish the game.

Team 17 was well-known, having recently published the commercially successful *Overcooked! 2* (2018) and *The Escapists 2* (2017). Team 17 was a rather fitting choice, too, considering the goofiness of many of their published games. They would be handling the marketing side of things for Rigerl and SMG.

Perhaps most importantly, SMG Studio started a large-scale playtesting circuit in 2019. They conducted over 150 different playtest sessions of *Moving Out* for over 120 hours of recordings. They also offered the game to play at a stand for fans to play at PAX (Penny Arcade Expo), a video game conference, to increase exposure and receive feedback.

In order to find "fresh" playtesters, *SMG* offered candy in exchange for high schoolers and local Facebook groups to play the games for them. "I think we went through probably two hundred bags of candy," Ashley Ringrose, CEO of SMG said in a *PlayStationBlog* interview.[290]

They recorded playtesters on Tuesdays and Thursdays, setting them up through resources like Calend.ly, and then

---

290 "How Playtesting Improved Moving Out, Out on PS4 Tomorrow," Play-
Station Blog, Sony Interactive Entertainment, April 27, 2020.

they'd post the records to YouTube to share with Rigerl and Team17.

Having so much playtesting allowed the developers to define the tone of *Moving Out*. One example is how characters and dialogue can convey different meanings. In game, players are able to jump through windows, shatter "sensitive" items, and launch items off cliffs. In an introduction of a level Team17 playtested, the player movers' boss initially just said: "The client said to not break their things." Though the developers had intended for this to be ironic, many of the playtesters took this seriously, and were careful not to break things.

When the development team added the lines "Just kidding! They paid for moving insurance. Smash all you want!," players were much more likely to do just that and have more fun in the process. Playtesting is important for this reason: it helps find problems of communication between the developers' intent and the players' understanding.

Putting so much effort into playtesting goes a long way. When I played the game, the tone of the "boss" dictated my entire perception and experience. In spite of playtesters being one of the most chronically underpaid roles in game development, I would argue that examples like these prove that they can make or break the game.[291]

By late 2019, the game was wrapping up development side. "The latest game, *Moving Out*, is almost finished now," Rigerl

---

291 Lottie Bevan, "British Game Dev Salaries," Weather Factory, July 17, 2020.

wrote on his blog.[292] And Team 17 had begun their far-reaching marketing campaign: posting a Reveal Trailer in August of 2019, posing itself as a "Mandatory Instructional Video" with '80s-style voiceover and art, welcoming listeners to the "Furniture Arrangement Relocation Technician ('F.A.R.T') family."[293] A similar trailer would be posted to Nintendo's official YouTube channel, garnering 170 thousand views (as of May 2020).[294] And on Steam, the team posted free demos of *Moving Out* in March to advertise for the release date on April 28, 2020.[295]

Moving Out was a commercial success. "8/10, a perfect for causing family arguments everyone can enjoy," *Metro UK* wrote.[296] "A must play for fans of same-screen multiplayer games," wrote IGN.[297] *Moving Out* was even included in *The Guardian*'s "Best Games of 2020 so far" list.[298] Overall, working with SMG Studios and Team17 ended up being the right decision, in terms of commercial success.

---

292 "Moving Out," Dev-M Games, December 12, 2019.

293 *Team17*, "Moving Out - Reveal Trailer (Nintendo Switch, PC, PS4 and Xbox One),"August 29, 2019, video, 1:09.

294 *Nintendo*, "Moving Out - Announcement Trailer - Nintendo Switch," March 17, 2020, video, 1:35.

295 "Moving Out," Steam, Valve Corporation, accessed August 25, 2020.

296 GameCentral. "Moving Out Nintendo Switch Review - Couch (and Fridge and TV) Co-op," *Metro*, April 24, 2020.

297 Tristan Ogilvie, "Moving Out Review," IGN, September 11, 2020.

298 Keza McDonald and Keith Stuart, "The Best Games of 2020 So Far," *The Guardian*, May 15, 2020.

Now that Rigerl's finished the development of *Moving Out*, and he has two supportive development and publishing teams, that means he must be done with this project, right?

Nope. Just like Barone and Persson, when I asked what his future plans are, he said he plans to continue working on *Moving Out*. He admitted that for *Moving Out,* there was a big section in the middle where it was just a lot of busy work that he didn't enjoy *too* much. Rigerl just didn't expect *Moving Out* to become quite this huge.

He continued that he "would also like to go back and make some smaller games again, because it's pretty rewarding." After the heavy lifting of creating such a large game, he'd like to make some smaller games again with the reward of a short development cycle.

As we've seen with many independent developers so far, money isn't necessarily their goal. Sure, it's convenient, it puts their games in the hands of more people, and it'll probably make their lives more financially comfortable. However, time and time again, we hear the same result: "I just want to make games. I don't care about the money."

With smaller games, you can see daily progress in your game development. It's the reward of seeing that your function you implemented is going to shave off a couple of megabytes of data off your GPU than your previous build, allowing you to include those shaders you've wanted to include for so long. It's the feeling when that buggy line of code finally *works.*

Still, it can be challenging to build a wildly successful game all by yourself, both in terms of development and commercial success. It's simply the trade-off we must make as independent developers: Do we risk low financial and developmental reward, or do we risk becoming just another cog in the machine?

CHAPTER 15

GETTING YOUR FOOT IN THE DOOR

"I definitely didn't [consider creating my own company right out of college]...I think that keeping that open mind really helps me to...explore other options that I hadn't considered, like games for education."

—DAKOTA HEROLD

Now that we've covered the stories of Eric Barone, Markus Persson, and Jan Rigerl as examples of independent game development, I'd like to bring the topic to a modern context. I want to take a look at a fresh face of game development, answering questions that many of you probably have about what it's like to enter the industry now, what starting up your own game development company is like, and what job stability is like.

In order to find the answer to these questions, I interviewed Dakota Herold, a student who graduated in 2017 from the Rochester Institute of Technology (RIT) in Rochester, New York. I was curious to hear about the experiences of a student in game development venturing into the game development industry, especially coming from a highly acclaimed school.

Herold is a game development programmer, but recently also a game development studio co-founder. He also serves on the board of RocGameDev, an established 501(c)(3) and community club in the city of Rochester, New York, that brings together game developers to support one another. He's suffered job losses and market instability, too. All in all, my questions for him were: How did you get to where you are now? What made you want to be where you are now?

Herold has loved games since he was young. Games like *Golden Axe* (1989) and *Sonic* games for the Sega Genesis were some of the first he ever played. During middle school, he played *Halo 3* (2007), a popular first-person shooter (FPS). That was around the time a major revelation came to him. "I don't know anything about making games, but making something like this is what I want to do for my career," he recalled to me during our interview. He surmised that he could learn game development in college.

Later, as he started applying to colleges, he looked at all his options for schools with decent game development programs. Though he'd said he'd wanted to work in the game development industry, and he planned to apply to a college through their game development program, he hadn't gotten his hands dirty (or…fingers typing?) in game programming, which was what he wanted to do. "I didn't really get into the process of developing and making games until I...got accepted at RIT, and kind of went from there. I wish I started earlier. Some of the people I talked to started [from] when they were playing games."

Herold hails from East Irondequoit, right out of Rochester, so his final decision ended up being local—he went with RIT. Other schools he looked at included some schools in California, which he described as feeling "out of reach." Herold applied early decision (to which he attributed the likely reason he got in) to RIT's game development program and got accepted to the class of 2017.

As Herold progressed through his degree in game development at RIT, he had many opportunities to work in the real world for companies in contract positions or internships. He worked as a student researcher at the game development school at RIT from 2015 until the end of his college career in May 2017, designing and implementing gameplay features for a medical education game in collaboration with doctors from the local University of Rochester Medical Center.

Herold's first job out of college was as a contract developer at Workinman Interactive, which he managed to land due to connections through RIT. Herold had worked with Professor Owen Gottlieb, a professor at RIT, on his game project called *Lost and Found*. Gottlieb wanted to bring on a professional project manager. One person Gottlieb chose to interview was Jason Arena, the founder of Workinman Interactive, a local game development company. Workinman has worked with many large companies such as Nickelodeon, Disney, and NBC Universal since its founding in 2002.

His role during Arena's interview involved showing Arena his own contributions to *Lost and Found*. Arena ultimately decided not to work on that project, but Herold left a good impression on him. When Herold graduated from RIT, he sent Arena a message—something along the lines of, "Hey, I'm graduating from RIT, I really enjoyed our conversation." "Next thing I know, I'm interviewing, and I'm starting to work at Workinman, you know what I mean?" Herold explained, with a hint of amazement in his voice.

FUN FACTS:

Games He's Worked On: *Dora the Explorer, Casa de Dora: New Adventures* (2017), *Bubble Guppies Halloween Party* (2017)

Game he would like to create: VR MMO that immerses you in some type of world, similar to *World of Warcraft*.

Companies Worked: Workinman Interactive, RNG Studios, Protagonist Games, Mythfire Studios

Favorite childhood games: *Golden Axe* (1989), *Halo 3* (2007)

When I asked Herold about the workplace culture at Workinman, he described it as an open floor plan. There was an upstairs area [where] he did concept development in brainstorming sessions and team meetings. He had his own workstation with a computer. He'd test his mobile web games on an iPad and an iPhone in the web browser to make sure that they worked.

There were also company-wide events, like social gatherings and get-togethers. They often had social events to celebrate holidays, like Halloween and Christmas. Add to that the fact that Workinman added some great professional names to Herold's resumé, like Nick Jr. on their intellectual property (IP) *Dora the Explorer* and *Bubble Guppies*, and you can see the way a young developer can get their foot in the door, while also making sure not to stretch themselves thin.

After Workinman, Herold got a job at RNG Studios full-time as a gameplay programmer in January 2018. There, he worked on RNG's games for two years. Unfortunately, Herold was laid off in January 2020 due to a large cutback at the company and he had to seek new employment. He made Twitter posts and posts on the RocGameDev Discord server asking for potential connections and opportunities to work in the game industry.

Luckily enough, Herold soon found a job at Protagonist Games, LLC, a startup game development company.

During this time, Herold also made the decision to cofound his own company, Mythfire Studios, as a way to have more creative freedom, apart from his employed work. On the team were Herold and Chris Driggers, both of whom have worked as game programmers professionally, as well as Taylor Fischer, a professional concept artist for video games.

Herold didn't expect to found his own company so quickly out of college. He had dream companies he wanted to work at but founding his own was not his original plan. "Keeping that open mind really helps to...explore other options. With all the experience that I've gotten, I've [been] exposed to a lot of different elements...of the industry. That's what secured this 'I know what I want to do when I [start] this company' mentality."

As an independent developer, Mythfire Studios does two things. For one, they contract work from publishers for their IP and game ideas and Mythfire helps realize them by developing the actual game. Second, they may also request funding from publishers to realize Mythfire's own IP and game design ideas.

When he first started out at Mythfire, the biggest thing was: How are we going to fund ourselves to be able to [work in game development]? They had decided early on not to hire anyone else and to contract as needed. It was important to establish rules and expectations as a startup company.

When I asked Herold whether these business and management concepts were things he learned at RIT, he said, "The program does a great job of introducing a new student to all the facets of game development, and then [moving those students towards] specialized courses...but they didn't have much in the way of 'What does the business of games look like?'" These entrepreneurial business and management ideals were things he learned on the job, rather than in college.

Mythfire's number one goal is to generate revenue so that they can keep going as a company. If they manage to make enough money on their first game, then they can get around to thinking about a second one—a similar challenge to that shared by David Cage when he started up Quantic Dream.

What's interesting is that Herold considered not even going to college and to teach himself game programming instead. He realized many online resources offered education of similar caliber for a fraction of the price. The only thing not included in those online resources, though, was network connections. That was one of the main reasons he attended college.

I have also lamented over the fact that hundreds, if not thousands, of free or low-cost alternatives exist to the American college model that teach game development. Websites like Udemy, Skillshare, YouTube, and Allison boast many high-quality courses for individuals at a price laughably cheap compared to universities in the United States—sometimes even being free.

Many who are in the industry today never studied in college anything related to what they do professionally. The divide becomes even more pertinent when you look at developers as a whole. A 2015 "Developer Survey" on StackOverflow, a site for computer developers, found that nearly half, or 41.8 percent of its developers, are self-taught.[299] Of them, 0.3 percent identified as game programmers; in 2019, 5.5 percent did.[300]

Still, Herold said, ultimately, "I'm glad…I met a lot of great people. That's what helped plant me where I am today." I must admit that networking is one of the most efficient ways to land a job. Sure, some of us manage to be the one in a million and land a bestseller like Barone did, but for most of us, meeting people already in the industry is the safest bet.

---

299 "2015 Developer Survey," Stack Overflow, accessed August 24, 2020.

300 "2019 Developer Survey," Stack Overflow, accessed August 24, 2020.

From our conversation, I learned a few things. For one, the industry is tumultuous. Layoffs and furloughs happen often, especially for the junior, fresher employees.

It's also often common for individuals to start up their own studio while also working at a company for pay, like Herold does. Yes, this means a lot more dedication and working hours. There's a trade-off that developers must make: go for the stability of a large company, but have less control creatively. The bigger the company, the less the control and the less variety in daily work life. However, it may mean more stability and better money.

If developers want more creativity, more control, they must sacrifice that stability and a lot of their time. They can work at a large company and do their own thing on the side, like Persson, or they can dive headfirst into the industry to do exactly what you want, with who you want, like Barone.

PART 4

HOW GAMES
GET MARKETED

CHAPTER 16

TODAY'S VIDEO GAME MARKETING LANDSCAPE

At this point in the book, we've covered the many avenues of work in the game development industry, from leadership, to employment, to indie game development. In this fourth and final section, I'd like to cover perhaps the most important question of all: how, exactly, are video games sold? How are they marketed to consumers?

The first time I saw an advertisement for a video game, it was for *Pokémon Diamond* (2007). As a child born into a half-Japanese, half-American household, I only viewed Japanese children's television shows, and many of them included advertisements for video games. The futuristic CG featuring the Pokémon running around in 3-D grasslands were more than enough to get me excited for the game. Soon enough I was watching the Pokémon TV show, buying Pokémon cereal, collecting Pokémon cards, and seeking out friends to play Pokémon with at school.

While this is a common story from children of my generation, it's really a showcase of effective marketing. Large companies like Nintendo, which partially owns *Pokémon* as its IP, will often funnel a significant amount of money into creating advertisements with mass-appeal to show off their games in the hopes that the targeted demographic will latch on. When you look at it from a (somewhat cynical) business perspective, I was just another successful catch.

While commercials on TV and radio were certainly popular for large companies, especially in the early 2000s, other methods of marketing started to grow in popularity. Why?

In the mid-2000s, online videos and livestreaming entered into popular culture. Before 2005, YouTube didn't exist. Before 2006, Twitch, the online livestreaming service, didn't exist either. But once these sites came into being, it would change just how we, as gamers, sought out which games to buy. Watching others play video games we wanted to play would become a highly profitable method of marketing games.

YouTube, now the video hosting giant and the second most popular search engine after Google (who also owns YouTube) was created by three former PayPal employees with the purpose of enabling video sharing with people all over the world.[301] Within a year, online gameplay videos started to crop up: from the *Pokémon* franchise to *Halo*, gamers

301 Adam Wagner, "Are You Maximizing the Use of Video in Your Content Marketing Strategy?," *Forbes*, May 15, 2017; Jefferson Graham, "Video Websites Pop Up, Invite Postings," *USA Today*, November 21, 2005.

wanted to show off new tricks they found in the games. Such videos were recorded with cameras that showed the glare of the screen, or with software like Bandi-Cam recorded the game from within the game software.

When I first discovered YouTube around 2006, one of the first things I latched onto was watching online gaming videos. That was actually what introduced me to watching Let's Plays (a style of video where the person filming plays the game while providing funny commentary or their thoughts while playing) and video game commentary videos, specifically on games like *New Super Mario Bros* (2006) and *Pokémon Mystery Dungeon: Red & Blue* (2006). I would stick with just one YouTuber at a time, watching Let's Plays that I enjoyed.

Once I finished a series, or was heavily invested in it, I would ask my parents to buy the game for me. If they acquiesced, I would play the game while continuing to watch the playthrough as a form of tutorial/entertainment. If my parents refused to buy the game, I would (jealously) watch the playthrough while imagining the different decisions I would make if I were the one playing the game. You can see how influential Let's Plays can be on young children. In fact, despite practically having only one friend who would play with me, I repeatedly chose the gaming and Let's Play videos over "real-life" friends.

YouTube was free, while other sites like Phanfare and Streamload used a subscription-based service and charged $6.95/month and $4.95/month, respectively.[302] In order to compen-

---

302 Ibid.

sate for offering a free service, YouTube put ads on videos. Google quickly bought up YouTube in 2006 for $1.65 billion, seeing potential in the company. Though YouTube was making $200 million per year for Google in 2008, by 2012, it was making around $3.7 billion.[303]

In 2007, YouTube launched its Partner Program (YPP), a system based on AdSense that allows the uploader of the video to receive a cut of the ad revenue, split with YouTube.[304] YouTube would take around 45 percent of the advertising revenue, while the uploader would receive 55 percent.[305] This meant you could *get paid* for recording yourself playing video games, a concept that many struggled to understand.

Around this time, the term "YouTuber" entered the lexicon: a term for somebody who created videos for entertainment purposes and treated it like a career. Back then, this word was almost derogatory, though now it is a rather common label.

People started posting videos of themselves playing all sorts of games en masse. This was the start of "Let's Players:" some of the biggest names being *Chuggaaconroy, PewDiePie,* and *UberHaxorNova.*

---

303 *Forbes,* "GooTube," May 29, 2008; Rolfe Winkler, "YouTube Growing Faster Than Thought, Report Says," *Wall Street Journal,* December 11, 2013, distributed by The Internet Archive Wayback Machine.

304 Tech Crunch, "YouTube Launches Revenue Sharing Partners Program, but No Pre-rolls," May 4, 2007.

305 Tim Carmody, "It's Not TV, It's the Web: YouTube Partners Complain about Google Ads, Revenue Sharing," The Verge, March 4, 2013.

The landscape has since shifted greatly over a decade later. In order to help you understand the scope of how much gaming-centered YouTubers can profit, here are some statistics of shifting demographics:

- Two billion users a month watched YouTube in 2019, up 5 percent from 2018[306]
- One billion hours of content is viewed every day[307]
- *Minecraft* is the most watched game on YouTube as of December 2019[308]
- Over fifty billion hours of YouTube gaming content was watched in 2018[309]
- YouTube ad revenue for 2019 was $15 billion[310]
- 96.5 percent of YouTubers make < $12,140/year (below the federal poverty line)[311]
- Top 1 percent of YouTubers receive 2.2 to 42.1 million views per month[312]

---

306 Todd Spangler, "YouTube Now Has 2 Billion Monthly Users, Who Watch 250 Million Hours on TV Screens Daily," *Variety,* May 3, 2019.

307 YouTube, "YouTube for Press," Google, accessed September 1, 2020.

308 *YouTube,* "YouTube Rewind 2019: For the Record | #YouTubeRewind," December 5, 2019, video, 5:36.

309 Dean Takahashi, "YouTube Gaming Videos Were Viewed for 50 Billion Hours in 2018," Venture Beat, December 8, 2018.

310 J. Clement, "YouTube: Share of Google Revenues 2017-2019," Statista, February 5, 2020.

311 Mathias Bärtl, "YouTube Channels, Uploads, and Views: A Statistical Analysis of the past 10 Years," Convergence: The International Journal of Research into New Media Technologies, Sage Journals, January 10, 2018.

312 Ibid.

- Markiplier, one of the top YouTube gaming personalities, made >$17.5 million in 2018[313]
- YouTubers make $0.35 to $5 per one thousand views[314]
  - Gamers are fourteen times more likely to be successful[315]
- YouTube channels generating > $100,000 rose 40 percent from 2016 to 2018[316]

As we can see, YouTube has clearly become a hotspot for content creators to earn money while playing video games and influence viewers to buy those games (hence the term "influencer"). The term "influencer" came into our lexicon around 2015, but really has only taken off since 2018.[317] As defined, it is one who or that which influences.

Video game companies would soon notice this fact, too, and learn to take advantage of it by sponsoring YouTubers to play their games. YouTube became a powerful way for companies to informally help sell their games without having to pay massive sums of money for ads to be displayed on websites or in TV commercials. Besides, those traditional methods were simply not as effective as this new form of advertising. And on top of YouTubers now being able to receive passive

313 Natalie Robehmed and Madeline Berg, "Highest-Paid YouTube Stars 2018: Markiplier, Jake Paul, Pewdiepie and More," *Forbes*, December 3, 2018.

314 Dmitry Gerasimenko, "Investor Money vs. Public Interest: Did Google Fail to Build a Non-evil Platform?," Medium, September 30, 2019.

315 Mathias Bärtl, "YouTube Channels, Uploads, and Views."

316 YouTube, "YouTube for Press."

317 "Influencer," Google Trends, Google, accessed September 1, 2020.

income from YouTube for ads being displayed on their videos, companies could also pay personalities directly to play their games for them—without those YouTubers being an official employee for that company.

Twitch, another platform that focuses on livestreaming services (as opposed to uploading pre-recorded footage), followed a similar track of history. It was started in 2007 by two tech entrepreneurs. It was originally known as Justin.tv, but rebranded itself as a purely gaming platform called Twitch in 2011.[318] Twitch was acquired by Amazon in 2014 for $970 million.[319] Like YouTube, Twitch has tens of millions of consistent viewers a month—as of 2017, Twitch had livestreamed 2.7 billion hours of content, or 72 percent of the market share of all livestreamed content online.[320]

Twitch would transform into another informal video game marketing platform, albeit a more focused one, compared to YouTube. Because much of the content on Twitch is focused on gaming (while YouTube harbors content aimed toward the general population), Twitch would attract advertisers from game development and publishing companies. Combine all this with the habits of the gamers themselves, and a new era of video game advertising was born.

318 Alex Wilhelm, "TwitchTV: Justin.tv's Killer New Esports Project," The Next Web, June 6, 2011.

319 Eugene Kim, "Amazon Buys Twitch for $US970 Million in Cash," Business Insider Australia, August 26, 2014.

320 Sarah Perez, "Twitch Continues to Dominate Live Streaming with Its Second-Biggest Quarter to Date," Tech Crunch, July 12, 2019.

The perks of Twitch don't end there; the fact that the content is live adds excitement for both the host and viewer. This creates the opportunity for the viewer to have a more vicarious experience and adds the desire to invest in the game and/or company. Though I was raised on YouTube, I must admit that the excitement created by a live show is unrivaled—like the difference between watching a movie versus a live performance.

Each platform contains more depth than I can possibly explore here, but the most important takeaway is that each of these platforms are industry leaders in connecting informal "gaming marketers" to companies and said company sponsorships. Premium programs like YouTube Red and Twitch Prime add complicated layers to each of these subjects, and each of these programs are constantly updating and changing.

How do marketing managers of video game companies interact with consumers now? What kind of marketing techniques do they use? How have some of these live streamers and online personalities made careers out of this?

The coming chapters will feature answers to these questions alongside interviews with marketing managers at gaming companies, such as Bethesda, Ubisoft, and Quantic Dream, which have worked with YouTube personalities like Markiplier and Lindsey Stirling to advertise games. Later chapters will also include interviews with Twitch streamers such as MissKyliee and TheSpudHunter, who have amassed dedicated audiences to their respective platforms, and speak to how they got into their current careers.

CHAPTER 17

THE POWER OF COLLABORATION

———

"I consider myself a digital native who still remembers what life was like before Twitter, and that place in between two eras of technology inspires me as a marketer every day. There are ways to leverage technology to tell stories clearly and simply, which to me is the hallmark of a good marketing and advertising campaign. I'm on Tik Tok, Instagram, Facebook, Snapchat, Twitter, VSCO, Reddit—you name it. I love to read peoples' opinions, love to see their take on things that are happening in the world, how they're reacting to a latest trend."[321]

—LISA PENDSE

———

[321] "Quantic Dream & Me - Interview with Lisa, Vice President of Marketing," Quantic Dream, February 27, 2020.

Did you know that beer and caffeine-laden energy drinks have sponsored e-sports events, or online/virtual gaming sports events? In 2018, Dr. Pepper, the soda brand, sponsored an e-sports team called TSM, and in 2019, Bud Light sponsored an *Overwatch* League competition.[322]

Energy drinks and alcohol being marketed to an audience that is nearly 25 percent teenaged raises questions of ethics.[323] As such, it's important for video game companies to be careful how they brand and market their games, lest they come under fire from unhappy consumers.[324]

Such marketing campaigns often call into question these practices, and it is important for marketing departments of video game companies to examine the ethics of their own actions. One individual who has exemplified such behavior is Lisa Pendse, vice president of marketing at Quantic Dream, who has previously worked at Sony Pictures and Ubisoft in advertising and marketing to sell video games and movies. She currently lives in Paris, France, as an employee at Quantic Dream. She has brought innovation and creativity to marketing for video games in ways that haven't been done before.

322　Andy Morton, "Dr Pepper Snapple Group Dives Deeper into E-Sports with Team Tie-Up," Just Drinks, January 22, 2018; Andy Morton, "Anheuser-Busch InBev's Bud Light to Sponsor eSports League," Just Drinks, May 2, 2019.

323　"Teen Online Vs. In Person Gaming Frequency in the U.S. 2015," Statista, August 6, 2015.

324　Lulu Chang, "Gamers are Being Targeted By Energy Drink Companies," Digital Trends, May 20, 2015.

Pendse never had dreams of working in the game development industry. She told me during our interview that when she was younger, she had a "perception of video games... [being] meant for boys, but that [she] could enjoy them too."

After graduating with a bachelor's in marketing and communications from Emerson College in 2004, Pendse got into producing marketing website collateral for sites like AOL and Sony Pictures. After working at Sony Picture Entertainment as a digital marketing executive in 2010, Pendse got into the video game industry in 2011 as a senior digital marketing manager for Ubisoft in San Francisco, California. Ubisoft is known for popular and best-selling game franchises like *Assassin's Creed* (2007-) and *Far Cry* (2004-).

"When Ubisoft came calling, I wasn't sure about it. I thought video games were just for young men who want to play violent games," Pendse described. There was a chance for the woman who would be Pendse's future boss to be a great mentor to Pendse, since she had also graduated from Emerson College.[325] And so she started her position at Ubisoft.

Because Pendse had mentioned to the manager that she had always wanted to live in a foreign country, it was a lovely coincidence that a few years into her time with Ubisoft San Francisco, a job opening appeared in Ubisoft's home office in Paris, France.

---

325 Youssef Maguid, "Women of Ubisoft - Lisa Pendse," Ubisoft, October 26, 2018.

"I was a bit nervous about it; it was a different role than I was in at the time. I had only been to Paris a couple times beforehand, and I didn't speak French," Pendse said about her decision. "It was quite a leap."[326] Having the support of her mentors, including that of her boss, helped.

The game she'd be working on would be *Just Dance 4* (2012), a mass-market casual party game, so she felt a lot more comfortable working on that than say, the next *Call of Duty* or *FIFA* (the former being a shooter-game, the latter being a sports game).

For *Just Dance 4*, the marketing team that Pendse worked with wanted to enlist the help of YouTubers. This happened back in 2011, when Twitch was just starting up, so they went with YouTube. Pendse explained to me how they'd reach out to the YouTubers. "[We'd contact them] either through their management, directly via email, or through third party, meaning an agency representing us...[The YouTubers] were always willing to entertain the idea of working together, but all creators I worked with had a pretty clear vision of their audience and their brand and would only agree to a concept if the game brand aligned with theirs."

One of these creators that Ubisoft worked with was Lindsey Stirling, a YouTuber who combines traditional violin, hip-hop, and dancing all together into one impressive show that somehow makes it all work. Her videos feature her playing a violin along an electronic musical backdrop, with impressive choreography on her part and cinematography on the

---

326 Ibid.

videographer's part. She has millions of subscribers (12.5 million, as of June 2020), and is quite a phenomenon within the online community. Several of her videos sport over one hundred million views.

In December of 2012, Stirling posted a music video to market *Just Dance 4*. By March 2020, it has received 8.8 million views. The video features Stirling dancing against a black backdrop with two other dancers, all three being outlined in the glowing white aura that surrounds dancers like in the *Just Dance* games. The screen looks just like the actual display for *Just Dance* gameplay as well, with the timing flashing and icons blinking in sync with the music that Stirling plays.

Ubisoft worked specifically with Lindsey Stirling to coordinate a video that wouldn't overtly scream "marketing," but also wouldn't miss the fact that it was trying to sell *Just Dance 4*—a fine line to walk. The video was highly effective. None of the YouTube comments mention that this is some cheap stunt to sell the game, and many in fact mention that they are disappointed that this song and dance were not in the actual game when it came out.

Just Dance 4 was a commercial success: it received a 77/100 from *Metacritic* and received the 2013 Favorite Video Game from the *Kids' Choice Awards*.[327] The strategies Pendse worked on had helped invigorate consumers who were

---

327 "Just Dance 4," Metacritic, CBS Interactive Inc., accessed September 2, 2020, distributed by The Internet Archive Wayback Machine; Jessica Derschowitz, "Kids' Choice Awards 2013: List of Winners," *CBS News*, March 23, 2013.

excited about their favorite hip-hop dance violinist taking the stage for a dance video game.

Another large project Pendse worked on was Ubisoft's E3 2017 presentation to promote *Just Dance Now* (2017), the mobile offshoot of the console game *Just Dance*, which features an impromptu dance battle in New York City, featuring dancers, actors, and songs played by trumpet players in the background.[328] Behind the scenes of the presentation were partnerships with Coca-Cola and Piccadilly Circus.

Coca-Cola provided a unique brand partnership, in which they gave Ubisoft the rights to use a song from their marketing campaign of the year in *Just Dance Now*. In exchange for that deal, Coca-Cola put QR codes directly on their cans in Europe to allow people to easily download the *Just Dance Now* (2014) mobile game directly onto their phones. This allowed more exposure of Coca-Cola's marketing campaigns for *Just Dance* players, and more exposure to *Just Dance* for Coca-Cola enthusiasts who happened to read the bottle. I've personally used similar services and can attest to their effectiveness, especially for games I'm excited about.

FUN FACTS:
Game she'd make with infinite resources: Wouldn't create a game, but a new type of technology disguising itself as a game. Would like to create a holodeck-level VR apparatus that doesn't physically encumber the user. Then, she'd

---

328 *GameSpot*, "Just Dance E3 Opening | Ubisoft E3 2018," June 11, 2018, video, 4:01.

create the most high-definition travel experience that lets people visit anywhere on the planet, and partner with game companies to gamify parts of the experience.

Games She's Worked On: *Just Dance 4* (2012), *Tom Clancy's Splinter Cell: Blacklist* (2013), *Detroit: Become Human* (2018)
Companies Worked: Sony, Ubisoft, Quantic Dream
Favorite Games: *FEZ* (2012), *Animal Crossing* (2001-), *Civilization* (1991-), *Stardew Valley* (2016)[329]

Videos such as these are great examples of the ways video game company marketing can work to integrate their product into advertising that will reach relevant audiences, aside from simply asking gaming personalities to play the company's games.

"I feel like they brought me [to France] because I had something special that they wanted and needed," Pendse said. "I do my best to make sure I'm giving it to them every day."[330]

Pendse continued in her position as international product marketing director at Ubisoft until 2019. By then, she had worked on titles such as *Tom Clancy's Ghost Recon Future Soldier* (2012) and *Tom Clancy's Splinter Cell: Blacklist* (2013), the traditionally "male," "violent" games that she had been wary of when entering the industry.[331] And having worked on games like *Just Dance* with women like Stirling to help promote the game, Pendse learned that games were for everyone.

---

329 "Quantic Dream & Me - Interview with Lisa," Quantic Dream.

330 Youssef Maguid, "Women of Ubisoft."

331 Ibid.

Video game series like *Animal Crossing* are the epitome of the fact that women can be just as involved in gaming as men, if not more, for certain types of games. *Animal Crossing: New Leaf* (2013) for the Nintendo 3DS features an impressive 56 percent female to 44 percent male userbase, in spite of the fact that 69 percent of total 3DS owners are male and 31 percent are female.[332] And Pendse, as somebody who loves the newest installment of the *Animal Crossing* series, mentions that playing such games are part of what helped her feel more comfortable in the industry.

Pendse then transferred over to Quantic Dream in 2019, where she now works as VP of marketing. Her roles include: "web, SEO ("search engine optimization"), CRM ("customer relationship management"), media, audience management, brand building, and live operations." There, she now works alongside minds like David Cage, CEO of Quantic Dream, and Ingrid Sanassee, motion kit lead at Quantic Dream to market games to the masses.

At Quantic Dream, one of Pendse's large projects was to market *Detroit: Become Human* (2018) for online streamers. Quantic Dream did not have much engagement with their community before *Detroit: Become Human*, so it was important that they expand their company's territory online.

On May 25, 2019, Quantic Dream unveiled "Quantic Stream," an inaugural livestream sharing information about Quantic

---

332   Nihon Keizai Shinbun, "任天堂・岩田社長が語る"本当の"ソーシャルゲーム" [Nintendo's President Iwata Talks about a "Real" Social Game], Nikkei, January 6, 2013.

Dream's projects, whose hosts would include David Cage, as well as Erika Ishii and Malik Forté, two well-known Twitch streamers and actors who have seventy-four thousand and twenty-eight thousand followers on Twitter, respectively. After they all shared Tweets about the Quantic Stream, viewership totaled around 1,500 people.

During the stream, many projects were presented to encourage viewers to participate and learn about the Quantic Dream brand. They gave away three signed copies of Quantic Dream games, announced the opening of their merch store, and also took questions from the audience, all done rather seamlessly thanks to the talented hosts, Erika and Malik, as well as a strong streaming support team running in the background.

Quantic Dream also implemented an online multiplayer system for *Detroit: Become Human* during the livestream that would allow Twitch streamers to collaboratively play with their viewers by using polls to decide which action to take, which would be built into the game itself. This encourages viewer retention and attention while watching Twitch streamers play the game.

Pendse called this endeavor a "labor of love" that she worked to make sure all the parts came together to share Quantic Dream's upcoming projects and branding in new and innovative ways.[333] And like her previous work of connecting Coca-Cola to advertising a video game with QR codes on the bottles, or working with the Piccadilly Circus to advertise *Just Dance Now*, there are many ways to advertise video

---

333 Lisa Pendse, Twitter post, May 18, 2020.

games without treading on unethical boundaries while still managing to catch eyes.

As a marketer for video games, she's evolved the job by collaborating with YouTube musicians and world-famous circuses. She's challenged marketing norms of simply running advertisements on TV or YouTube. And by working in the video game industry directly, as well as games that welcome the female demographic, she's learned that the industry isn't as antagonistic toward women as she previously thought.

CHAPTER 18

THE MODERN STAGE

"It was a little bit like the Wild West, but there was—I would say that there was a real feeling that [online streaming/gameplay] was a big new medium, and it wasn't like television. It was something different than that."

—SEAN BAPTISTE

You wouldn't think that being a playwright would make you a good marketer for a brand. Sure, being able to write and act for plays might let you come up with some great one-liners for a brand or possibly market the brand yourself in some commercials, but generally you'd assume you need some business skills that you learned beforehand to be able to take up such a role.

When it comes to marketing for gaming companies, as we've discussed, many traditional norms for marketing are flipped; advertising on TV with your target demographic enjoying the product you're selling just doesn't cut it anymore. Video game marketers now need to make sure they connect with gamers in a relevant way. That's what Sean Baptiste saw coming from a decade ago.

Baptiste, now influencer marketing manager at Bethesda, manages relationships with streamers in order to have them play Bethesda's games, such as *The Elder Scrolls V: Skyrim* (2011) and *Doom* (1993-). He now boasts just under eleven thousand followers on Twitter and amasses several hundred viewers per Twitch stream. But he didn't just fall into the role—he faced a long journey before he even considered such a position.

Baptiste started off studying theater at Bradford College in Haverhill, Massachusetts, in 1996, with a great love and passion for all things acting, stage play, and playwrighting. He studied theater and history but was unable to obtain a degree because the school closed in 2000. He struggled soon after when he found out that he had a brain tumor that would require him to be hospitalized. For several months, the procedure and recovery prevented him from pursuing theater-related jobs because they would be too physically demanding for him.

So, most of his days after graduation were spent in recovery. "All I did was stay in my house and just play video games. I couldn't do theater anymore," he explained to me in our interview.

This game-playing rabbit hole led Baptiste to consider games as a career aspiration in some form or another. "[In] video games…you're the performer and the audience," he said. He began to see a similarity in the living relationship between the audience and the game or the play. "Theater is not like film in one very important aspect: no matter how prescribed the play is, there's still a relationship between the audience—a living relationship—between the audience and the performer. That's what video games are, except in a really weird way."

As his recovery continued, he had to start thinking about how to get a job. But just because Baptiste clicked with video games, that didn't necessarily mean that he could walk into any company and ask for a job. He had to find a way to brand what he'd learned as something useful to a gaming company. And so he found the way by offering a unique take on marketing—not in the traditional, business suits and pointing-at-graphs sense, but rather by connecting companies with online forums and communities to sell games at a grassroots level.

In 2005, Baptiste started working at the small indie video game development studio, Harmonix. He started out as a QA tester, then worked up to a position as a community manager in 2007, during which he built up a community department and acted as manager to direct a messaging forum with fans, establish customer service, and manage events. He showcased their games, like *Guitar Hero* (2005). Then he moved onto Wicked Smart Kids Productions in 2010, where he produced material for the television pilot *When I Grow Up*, a show about recovering from a traumatic brain injury. He briefly returned to Harmonix in 2012 to work on community building.

It was in 2012, when he moved on to working for Fire Hose Games, that he started to dip his toes in the water of "influencer" management. While his job technically covered a mixture of community management, marketing, and PR for their games, he saw potential in contacting Twitch streamers to help market Fire Hose's games. "We didn't have any money to market our games...so we had to find ways to do it ourselves," he explained. YouTube and Twitch were just starting to boom with gaming content being posted more and more, so it was easy to see the potential for connecting gaming content creators with gaming companies for a new type of advertising.

Baptiste would simply reach out to them with a message, introducing himself and asking if the streamer would like a free key to play their game on stream. "It was a little bit like the Wild West, but there was...a real feeling that this was a big new medium, and it wasn't like television. It was something different than that." During this time, he also started up the Fire Hose Games channel on Twitch, which received four million views by the time he left in 2015.

An exchange occurs here: the streamer receives a free game (usually between $20 and $60) to play on stream, as well as the feeling of being able to help a small game studio. The game company hopes that the streamer playing their game raises awareness and builds community interest in their game—similarly to what happened to Eric Barone's *Stardew Valley* and Markus Persson's *Minecraft* post-launch. Sometimes, the game company will pay the streamer, but this is rare, and usually saved for highly popular streamers (who will be able to influence tens of millions of people) from highly successful game studios (like EA or Blizzard).[334]*

FUN FACTS:

Games He's Worked On: *Rock Band* (2007), *Doom Eternal* (2020)

Game he would like to create: A game based on the movie *Tremors* (1990) with asynchronous multiplayer. Team A plays as humans trying to avoid the sand pits where the worms are, in a standard third person FPS. Team B plays as the worms without any visuals, using only 3-D surround sound auditory cues to find the humans.

Companies Worked: Harmonix, Fire Hose Games, Adult Swim Games, Bethesda

Favorite Games: *Ms. Pac Man* (1982), *Zork I* (1980), *Doom* series (1993-)

Marketing in this way started off as both a challenge and an opportunity. While it kept costs down, it was sometimes challenging to find people who were willing to play their games. "[The job was about] finding some people who are into the concept of the game, then making them feel like part of the whole development of it," he explained to me.

---

334 * This is also a hotly debated form of game promotion. Now, due to legislation passed by the Federal Trade Commission in the United States, YouTubers and streamers must tell viewers at some point during their video that the game (or product) they are showing is sponsored. Still, creators who do too many sponsored videos tend to get a bad rep for "selling out."

"Like they're part of something bigger and can help make something bigger. Something that they actually care about."

Baptiste's methodology follows the more accepted convention of organic promotion over compensated promotion. Baptiste aimed to build organic relationships with streamers where, at a fundamental level, they were gamers enjoying a game—that just so happen to do so in front of a camera, as an actor does on stage in theater.

The position that Baptiste was coming from was unique: a playwright without a completed degree and a love for video games who wanted to combine those two worlds. I don't think it's possible for him to have found a better combination. It wasn't only a "thinking-outside-the-box" mentality that he naturally had as an actor—it was also an ability to apply that to the video gaming medium with an eye for business and find a compelling way to leverage his knowledge of acting into an informal, video game-related business model that also builds a relationship with viewers.

I can speak from personal experience that watching others play games has only incentivized me, personally, to invest in the company; if not their games, then their merchandise. However, I've found that this style of marketing is most effective for games where each playthrough will yield different results: think *Minecraft*, *Stardew Valley*—but not so effective for games with one single storyline, like the *Uncharted* series or *Assassin's Creed* series.

I often feel after watching story-driven games that I now don't need to play the game myself—just like Amy Hennig also observed. On the other hand, games with randomization are able to create an entirely new experience each run-through, incentivizing me, as the stream/video viewer, to go and play it myself.

Anyway, back to Baptiste. His most recent position since 2018 has been at Bethesda Softworks, where he works as a senior public relations ('PR') and streaming manager. In this position, he has perhaps worked with the biggest names thus far and therefore led the most successful marketing campaigns.

In January 2020, Baptiste went on a "road tour" of sorts to visit Markiplier, one of the most successful YouTube gaming personalities. He also met up with T-Pain, a famous rapper-turned-Twitch streamer, to play Bethesda's newest hit, *Doom Eternal* (2020). Both Markiplier and T-Pain would play the game on camera together with Baptiste and a partner from Bethesda. Both are known fans of the *Doom* series, which has existed as a hyper-successful, hyper-violent first-person shooter (FPS) video game series since 1993.

"Just being able to do things a little bit more in more of an intimate space, as opposed to...renting a space and then having a whole bunch of people come in, it was more one on one," he explained. Instead of inviting Markiplier and T Pain to a "Bethesda" booth at a game conference, Baptiste figured that having these personalities play Bethesda's games in their very own homes, where they usually stream, would allow for the most "organic" gameplay of *Doom Eternal,* and both of their personalities would really shine.

Baptiste was right: Markiplier's *Doom Eternal* videos have raked in an average of over two to three million views per video on YouTube (as of September 2020).[335] Assuming each view is equal to one viewer, Markiplier's viewer count is enough to fill just over eighteen University of Michigan football stadiums, which houses 107 thousand fans. And when I imagine that many versions of a younger me, begging my parents to buy the cool new game I saw on YouTube, it's easy to imagine how effective and relatable this kind of marketing campaign can be. The fact that it's a video where the viewer is an audience member that gets to vicariously experience gameplay compounds that over television and online ads that are fleeting and non-immersive.

Baptiste's background in theater is unique in two ways: it gives him experience with being the performer *and* it gives him experience with responding to an audience. With this in mind, he's able to understand what the careers of streamers are really like. He's also able to be the performer, too, at times, on his own streams.

Baptiste also mentioned that it's difficult to ignore the work that he, as an influencer manager, asks of these (often young adult) influencers. Many are teenagers or in their early twenties who are essentially their own business owners and single-handedly building a brand. "It's performance for sometimes eight to twelve hours a day. A lot of them we talk to, they're working sixteen-hour days," he described to me about their work culture. They're also often isolated, forced

---

335 *Markiplier*, "1 Vs 1,000,000 | Doom Eternal - Part 1," March 20, 2020, video, 1:26:49.

to put on a happy face at times when they're not all too happy. "That's really, really hard," Baptiste lamented. "I really do care about their mental health."

He takes that into account for himself, too. He's built up a large following on Twitter by performing for Bethesda livestreams to play their games like *Doom Eternal* and *Skyrim*, and I asked him about the performative nature of the shows he hosts. "I think back in the day, I probably would put on more of a face," he said, "But as I've gotten older, and probably a bit more cynical, I think I'm more comfortable just being like, 'Look, this is just who I am...I love showing people stuff. Like, oh...check this out!'"

The new marketing landscape for video games is changing in ways we couldn't have imagined before, and it's come with new consequences and benefits we couldn't foresee a decade ago. But at its core, this is a booming new medium that, in some regards, is proving far more successful than traditional TV advertisements.

So how exactly do live streamers operate? As an informal type of free or paid marketing for video game companies, how have they managed to make careers out of playing games for an audience? What are their livelihoods, and do they have any relationships with the video game companies whose titles they spend hours on end playing?

CHAPTER 19

GAMING FOR A LIVING

"Because of Twitch as a whole, the gaming industry as a whole, streaming as a whole, even my community, the way they shaped me, making me more open and making me more loving and just having all the support from [my audience]...it kind of changes you, but in a good way...It changed me in a way where I felt safe. I felt comfortable telling people my story."

—MISSKYLIEE

MissKyliee, or "Kylie," as she often goes by, was still in her undergraduate years at Collin College in McKinney, Texas, when her father told her: "You talk to yourself while gaming—you might as well do it in front of an audience."[336] Back in 2013, streaming to a live audience was unique, with most

---

336 "About MissKyliee," MissKyliee, accessed September 4, 2020.

gaming content mostly being housed on Let's Plays on You-Tube. Like Baptiste noted, streaming for a live audience is more organic and would allow her to build a connection with viewers. Plus, she could make money this way, too.

She considered opening a Twitch account for several months. She watched Twitch streamers to find out how they ran their shows and how Twitch worked and, in August 2013, alongside the official re-release of *Final Fantasy XIV* (2013), one of her favorite games, she finally decided to start Twitch streaming.

"I really started from nothing," she said to me during an interview. It was "magical" seeing an audience gathering to watch her. She would play a day or two a week at first, but she started to see growth rather quickly. People were interested in seeing her content while playing the newest *Final Fantasy* game and they stuck with her for her entertaining persona. Eventually, Kylie was partnered on Twitch in January 2014, allowing her to accept subscription and ad revenue. She started to consider going full-time.

However, on April 3, 2014, Kylie's father passed away due to suicide. "It was a huge shock to me and my family. I don't know how I even finished up that semester in college...but I did," Kylie explained. She stepped away from streaming to cope for a couple of months, but eventually, she returned.

At first, she couldn't tell her audience about her loss in spite of the break she'd taken. She was still processing her grief and loss. Yet she found the streams became her way of managing it. Her stream always made her feel better at the end of the day, and looking back, it was the way she processed the loss of her father. In January 2015, she decided to go full-time with her Twitch streaming career.

"My father always loved seeing me stream and always thought it was the coolest thing," she described, "so in a way it boosted my motivation to go full time." A couple days before her father passed, she recalled that she told him how she had been planning an April Fools stream to make her audience laugh; "I hadn't seen him laugh that hard in months. [It was a] bittersweet memory though, because that [was] the last time I ever saw my dad." His memory and his support of her endeavors encouraged Kylie to pursue livestreaming.

Money can be difficult and unstable for a Twitch streamer. Yes, it can look like a dream career where you make money from people watching you just play video games, but in reality, it's a lot more involved than that. Twitch streamers who make a livable income are the top of the top, which does not reflect the reality of most streamers.

To put it into context: if the streamer has two thousand consistent viewers every stream for a month, then they will make around $2,000 from streaming revenue alone, split with Twitch, according to *Forbes*.[337] Only the top few streamers may break $100,000 per year in revenue. Most rely on sponsorships and establishing a brand through social media to make a living. At one hundred thousand followers and counting, Kylie must still rely on sponsorships and brand deals to rely on Twitch streaming as a source of income.

---

337 Cameron Keng, "Online Streaming and Professional Gaming Is a $300,000 Career Choice," *Forbes*, April 21, 2014.

FUN FACTS:

Game she would like to create: An MMORPG like *Final Fantasy XIV* (2013) series, *MapleStory* (2005), *Mabinogi* (2004), and *Aion* (2008) with housing, decorating, cool combat, and raids all included. She's always loved MMOs and RPGs but wishes she could take all the favorite individual aspects of each game and "Frankenstein" them together.

Favorite Games: *The Legend of Zelda: Majora's Mask* (2000) and *The Legend of Zelda: Breath of the Wild* (2017)

Kylie has built affiliate sponsorship relationships with companies like Amazon and SteelSeries, a pro gaming gear store. As an example of how affiliate sponsorships work, a fan of Kylie's may purchase gear for themselves using a code shared by Kylie. A percentage of the revenue goes to the influencer, and the fan themselves receives a 10 percent discount for purchasing through the sponsorship. Therefore, the fan has incentive to use this code because not only do they get a sale, they also get to support a creator they're a fan of. The sponsoring company also gets more promotion because a public figure like a Twitch streamer is promoting their products. It's rather simple how this form of new marketing that has only popped up in the last five years is groundbreakingly lucrative. I've personally used such codes to purchase products to support online creators, and it makes me feel like I'm contributing to their cause, which is a great feeling.

Kylie has also established promotional brand partnerships, where she receives a designated amount of money for promoting a brand on stream. She mentioned that she was approached by Hot Pocket to promote their products on stream—something she was very happy about.

Another option streamers have is to sell your brand merchandise. Many Twitch streamers and online gaming personalities on YouTube, such as PewDiePie, have large online storefronts with "drops"—a line of clothing that "drops" at a specific date or time with limited supply, creating a sense of exclusivity—and use the merch to make a living. Merch tends to include things such as clothing, drink bottles, and electronic device cases. However, Kylie does not have any merch that she sells, though she plans to in the future.

Of course, there are also donations during live streams. Twitch is set up in a way where you can "sub" to a streamer for either $4.99/month, $9.99/month, or $24.99/month or subscribe to them for free with an Amazon Prime membership (as you may recall, Twitch was bought out by Amazon in August 2014 for $970 million). The streamer, on average, receives half of the cut.[338] Viewers may receive special privileges such as a badge icon next to their name in chat, access to ad-free viewing of the stream, and access to channel-exclusive emoticons.

A Twitch streamer's fans may also just straight up donate money. This may be in the context of donating to the streamer directly, similar to tipping a waitress, which is often exciting to watch as a viewer as it adds a sense of live support to the creator you are watching.

---

338 "How to Subscribe," Twitch, Amazon, accessed September 4, 2020.

Another option is donating during a charity livestream. Often, Twitch streamers will designate a certain timeframe ("24 Hours") as a "Charity Donation" livestream day, where all donations will be donated directly to a charitable cause, such as a cancer walk or mental health charity. These "Charity Livestreams" tend to be very popular because viewers are able to watch the streamer's reaction to large donations.

One of Kylie's most notable charity livestreams that she did was for the American Foundation for Suicide Prevention (AFSP) on June 17, 2015. Her initial goal was to reach $2,400 within the twenty-four-hour time limit. Within one minute of starting the stream, a viewer named Andrew donated $2,500. Less than an hour later, a viewer named Brevlo donated $3,000. To each donation, she was struck to near tears.[339] On multiple other occasions, some donors supplied sums in the thousands; however, that's not to say every other donation is less important or meaningful.

By the end of the twenty-four-hour stream, Kylie had raised over $37,000. Perhaps most importantly, she shared the story of her father's suicide on stream. Though she was in tears, her chat was filled with positive messages of support.

These charity livestream videos tend to be wildly popular, especially with YouTube compilations of their "best" reactions. It's with good reason—not only is it exciting to see the total sum of money be donated to a good cause, but as viewers, we can see the reactions of the streamer, from the grateful to the speechless, to sometimes absurd amounts of

---

339 *Miss Kyliee*, "24 Hour AFSP Charity Stream," June 17, 2015, video, 22:18.

money. These charity livestreams are a wonderful example of the good that Twitch and streaming culture, in general, can do.

"I didn't honestly think that by...creating that charity, that big of an impact would have happened," Kylie said. "Still to this day...I hear people...saying thank you for [hosting that stream]."

In late 2017, Kylie also began to pursue a BS in marketing at the University of Texas Dallas. She dropped her streaming hours from full-time to part-time to compensate for the time needed to study, but she still kept up with streaming at night and on weekends.

After graduating UTD, she got a job as a marketing coordinator for a company that has relationships with gamers. She still works around twenty hours a week, and she intends to keep streaming around for as long as she can—"It's too much fun!"

Kylie, who doesn't give out her full name or age (though this changed in April 2020 when she revealed she turned thirty) for the sake of her own privacy, has built up a large brand around herself. "Honestly, it's bigger than myself some of the time," she told me. She calls herself and her Twitch brand the "Fairy Family" and has a personal website that links all of her social media profiles in one place.

It is entirely possible to separate business life from personal life and to keep streaming as strictly "business" while also keeping it fun. While Kylie says she tries to be her authentic self, it was initially difficult to not keep relationships going with her first few fans. "I felt almost like I…owed them, you know? They're supporting me, they're always here for me. I need to be there for them too."

She would often stay up every night using apps like Teamspeak, then services like Discord, to chat with the twenty-plus people who hung around after her streams. "My business and my personal life got so interwoven that it was really hard to just shut off." Eventually, she had to take a step back from chatting with her fans, because it was affecting her mental health. "Streaming is a personal job," Kylie said. "But it's important to set those boundaries."

At the end of the day, though, her fans are the greatest part of the experience as a streamer. "I still get amazed every time I…go live, and there's one hundred or more people there in chat just waiting for me," she said while laughing. "I mean, obviously I must be doing something right for them to keep coming back and always [say] hi."

Being a Twitch streamer is becoming more and more an integral part of the gaming business. After all, without YouTube, Twitch, or many of the other streaming options out there, many of us would've never heard of the games we play today—especially the independent studios, because so many of them lack the advertising power that large companies do. Streaming is a wonderful way, as Baptiste also found out, to not only promote games "for free" (from the company's end) but also to give visibility to games developed by groups without enough money to spend on advertising.

However, there's still push back against "playing video games in front of a camera" being a legitimate job. From Kylie's experiences, we can see the influence that such streamers can have over people. Aside from informally helping to market games, streamers can also give people a community where they can share their interests or discuss topics with stigmas that they wouldn't otherwise feel comfortable discussing.

Livestreamed gaming is a new form of community building and marketing. It was vital to helping sell *Stardew Valley* by Barone and it has helped exposure for developers like Rigerl and Persson and marketers like Pendse. Game development companies, charities, gamers, and non-gamers who enjoy watching streams can all take advantage of this fact, to share the products, games, and experiences we have.

CHAPTER 20

GAMING FOR A LIVING, 2

___

"I have a bit of a go-with-the-flow attitude to[wards Twitch streaming]...it's like busking...I'm at the mercy of people's generosity, so it can feel a bit all over the shop with the income, but...I've shifted [streaming] into a full-time gig."

—THESPUDHUNTER

"FPS Sweatlord." "Sweaty Competitive FPS Gamer with a twist." "Professional Clown." When it comes to all things career-wise, I'm sure most people in the world would be horrified to submit a resumé to an employer with these taglines right under their name. Most of us tend to have a strict work life/social life separation, and while these taglines are ways you might jokingly refer to yourself on a late-night chat with friends, we would never call ourselves these names to our boss's face.

In the Twitch streamer industry, though, they're just parts of a self-created identity; a brand developed from several years of playing video games for an audience. And that's exactly how TheSpudHunter came up with these phrases to brand himself, and why all of his social media features these taglines in a scratched-up-looking red and yellow font.

Let me back up a little bit. "TheSpudHunter," or "Spud/Spuddy" as he often goes by, is a professional, full-time, Australian Twitch streamer. He comes from a small part of South Australia called Adelaide, which Spud describes as a "very quiet town."

He previously worked as a contractor for a store, where he felt finances were out of his control. "[If the company] loses contracts, it has nothing to do with me," he explained. "[I was] at the mercy of my bosses." It frustrated him to not have control over how he made money.

However, when he was streaming, he was able to become his own boss—though he never intended for it to be that way. "I've always loved gaming and I [started streaming] for a laugh, and then somehow it started gaining momentum," Spud explained to me. He appreciated the fact that unlike working under somebody else, he could control his own schedule. Plus, streaming as a profession has a meritocratic nature: the more work you put into it, the more opportunity you have to reap the rewards.

Spud started Twitch streaming in December 2017. He's kept a rather steady schedule when it comes to streaming; he considers it highly important to being successful. Halfway through 2018 was when he began to realize, "All right. This is what I'm going to do full-time."

He often plays games from the *Doom* series (1993-) and *Quake* series (1996-) both created by Bethesda, and fast-paced first-person shooter (FPS) games. His Twitch streams run almost every day, and he regularly has several hundred audience members. Spud has always loved FPS games, like *Doom,* ever since he was young. In fact, when I asked him what the first games he ever played were, he responded, "Still *Doom* and *Quake,*" with laughter.

Doom and *Quake* are famous game series that started in the late '90s era with a focus on FPS and a gritty, violent aesthetic. *Doom* is an iconic franchise that first started in 1993. The first title in the series, *Doom,* popularized new technologies that hadn't really broken into the mainstream yet. 3-D graphics, the reliance on 3-D space, multiplayer gameplay, and player-created modifications (or "mods") were all ground-breaking techniques that solidified *Doom*'s place in history.

The franchise has since come out with twelve games in the series, with its most recent installment, *Doom Eternal,* released in March 2020.[340] It has been praised for its graphics, gameplay, and soundtrack, and sold an estimated seven hundred thousand copies on Steam in its first week, making it the best-selling Steam game of 2020 (as of March 2020).[341]

---

340 Samuel Stewart, "Doom Games In Order," GamingScan, July 12, 2020.

341 Littledinamit, "Doom Eternal Rips and Tears Through Competition, Sells Over 700K on Steam," PlayTracker, March 29, 2020.

Quake was developed by id Software and published by GT Interactive in 1996. The reason for its acclaim comes from its success in being one of the few games that offered full real-time 3D rendering with support from OpenGL ("Open Graphics Library"), a programming interface for rendering 2D and 3D graphics, which came into existence in June 1992. It was released as a spiritual successor to the *Doom* series. The main purpose of its creation was to enhance *Doom*'s multiplayer by adding online multiplayer and *QuakeSpy*. *QuakeSpy* is a software that makes the process of distributing mods of *Quake* and sharing servers with other players online safer. "Think of *Quake* like *Doom* but a lot faster," Spud explained. *Quake* was also the result of a collaboration with Trent Reznor of Nine Inch Nails, a well-known American rock band in the '90s. He supplied the soundtrack and sound effects free of charge.[342]

One of the coolest things Spud has experienced in his career as a Twitch streamer is being able to visit the United States and game conferences. QuakeCon, a conference dedicated to *Quake*, one of Spud's favorite games, holds a special place in his heart. "I have a very strong relationship with Bethesda because I'm very passion about the IPs that they own, particularly the first-person shooters," Spud described. QuakeCon was where he met Sean Baptiste, who introduced me to Spud.

When it comes to the finances of being a Twitch streamer, Spud described to me, "I have a bit of a go-with-the-flow attitude to it...it's like busking." Sure, there's no strictly

342   Evan Minsker, "Nine Inch Nails' 1996 *Quake* Soundtrack Gets First-Ever Vinyl Release," Pitchfork, September 17, 2020.

established contracts, and oftentimes subscribers who provide a small, yet steady, source of income will drop their support. "I'm at the mercy of people's generosity, so it can feel a bit all over the shop with the income, but...I've shifted it into a full-time gig."

Still, he doesn't like to think of streaming as a "job" or as a means of getting money. He tries not to think about the money side of things and doesn't love doing sponsored streams. "I haven't been too aggressive in chasing that because I've felt that personally, the more sponsored streams I do, I feel like my community'll think I'm making a lot of money." He considers himself a "very lucky" person that his viewers donate a livable amount to support him.

"I'm just always very thankful to them," Spud said. "Not in an over-the-top manner, but more of in a genuine sort of, 'Hey, without you guys, [I] couldn't do this.'"

When thinking about the future, Spud still wants to continue streaming until he can't anymore. It's true that some things are hard to account for; working in entertainment as *the* entertainer tends to be one of the more unsteady career paths to lead compared to something like working in accounting. "I'll just keep going at it and developing what I do," he said. "Just see where the road takes me. I really enjoy it."

Spud is also trying to build up a YouTube channel alongside his Twitch channel by creating video guides on *Doom Eternal*. Spud's "Ultra Nightmare Guide" (a mode in *Doom Eternal* which only gives the player one life—once you die, you have to start from the beginning of the game, and enemies are much more deadly) was featured on the Slayer's Club in April 2020, a community forum section of Bethesda's official website.[343] The video itself has received over 110 thousand views as of June 2020.[344]

Features by the companies whose games you play can be a great launching pad for an online content creator. In just one week, Spud's YouTube channel has gained one thousand subs, putting him at seven thousand total as of April 2020.[345] It's clear that Bethesda's feature gave him a boost in subscribers and supporters of his brand.

FUN FACTS:
Game he'd play, given infinite resources: Still *Doom* and *Quake.*
Favorite Games: *Doom* series (1996-), *Quake* series (1993-)

Overall, Spud is still putting in his best efforts to becoming successful as an online streamer and content creator. "I just try and keep the CPM (content per minute) high, and keep them laughing, and keep doing what I do."

---

343 *TheSpudHunter*, "Ultra Nightmare Guide and Tips for Doom Eternal," April 6, 2020, video, 20:54.

344 Jonny Roses, "Conquer Ultra Nightmare With This In-Depth Guide," Bethesda Softworks, April 17, 2020.

345 *TheSpudHunter*, YouTube Channel, accessed September 21, 2020.

When taking a look at Spud's time as a Twitch streamer, it's important to realize the value in networking. Without networking, he wouldn't have had the chance to attend QuakeCon or meet Sean Baptiste, who I met (again, through networking myself for this book), which gave him ties to Bethesda. By regularly connecting with Bethesda's accounts and employees through social services like Twitter, he's able to build up a network for himself for future contracts and sponsorships, and even just make friends with the developers of a game franchise he loves (which is great in and of itself).

Of course, it's also important to reflect on his attitude toward streaming and being an online personality. Spud himself said that his persona while streaming is almost exactly the same as his real self. While many of us are aware of the distinction between an actor and their acting roles, with being an influencer who is always online, always putting up a persona, the topic of mental health has been in the spotlight for these influencers in recent years. We've grown more used to hearing about influencers and online personalities burning themselves out because they have to put up a facade in front of the camera.

For Spud, Sean, and Kylie, they mentioned how there's little distinction between their on-camera selves and off-camera selves. While it's important to keep a schedule with maintaining an audience as a Twitch streamer, it's also important to be honest and tell them when you need a break. Perhaps keeping that distinction between your real self and your on-camera self subtle is the key to maintaining a healthy relationship between yourself and your career as a streamer.

Online personalities are a new field of marketing that has sprung up in the past decade. We don't know what direction that it will move in, but one thing is for certain: the connection and "informal sales" it gives to games are invaluable.

CONCLUSION

——

There's a lot that goes into the development of a game. And by development, I hope you now understand that it's not just about programming or just about business; it's also the marketing, the user-centric design, and the relatable influencers. It is the independent developers and the publisher-centric developers. These core concepts are fundamental to understanding today's video game development landscape.

When I first started writing this book, I knew I wanted to get every possible perspective on video game development that I could. I wanted to dispel notions that anybody involved in the video game industry is an awkward programmer or money-hungry businessperson; that designers are less important than programmers; or that online gaming streamers are an illegitimate job, to name just a few stereotypes. I hope that I have shown you that, while video games are a business, there are people and careers behind almost every part of its interconnected framework. They all give life to this industry.

Almost everybody involved in this book was a gamer as a child save for a few who happened to discover video games later in life. My hope in pointing out peoples' favorite games as "fun facts" was not simply for the novelty of finding out such information, but to help you understand what games influenced people to join the game industry. Some found the puzzles in the game to be striking, and that sparked their interest in game design. Others found the animations intriguing, and that set them on a path towards animating for video games. Perhaps looking into your own past could illuminate a future career choice.

However, that doesn't mean that unless you are familiar with all aspects of gaming, you cannot enter the video game industry. It's important to acknowledge that while being familiar with gaming—both its culture and industry—is helpful in steering individuals toward the game industry, having a strong skill (marketing, programming, design) can often cover for that lack of familiarity when first dipping your toes in. The game industry is welcoming to all, despite the accusations of exclusion we hear about in the news.

Another fact I wanted to emphasize is how interconnected the game industry is. It's difficult to find somebody who *only* programs or *only* manages the business side of things. Because of the inherent nature of the industry, it's difficult to market games without having firsthand experience of playing them yourself. It's difficult to program the game without understanding the fundamentals of music, physics, animation, and game design. And it's quite difficult to create art for the game without understanding how every cog of the game development machine works. When you enter the video game industry, no matter how you came in, you'll likely end up as a versatile team player.

Many of the stories I've presented reflect this. While David Cage became a story writer and manager of his own company, he was a musician at heart and incorporated what he had learned as a musician into his games. Sean Baptiste was a playwright but figured out how to turn acting into a marketing strategy for video game companies. Hidetaka Miyazaki was a disgruntled businessman who went against cultural norms to become a programmer and then a designer on one of the most notoriously difficult and critically acclaimed games of today.

Speaking of interconnectedness, I couldn't go on without mentioning networking. Networking was fundamental to creating this book. Without it, I would've lacked the personal stories I heard from conducting the interviews I was privileged to land. The game development industry has very friendly people, and many conversations that I was nervous to have ended up being welcoming and pleasant. Networking is invaluable in helping you land opportunities that you wouldn't have gotten otherwise. Unfortunately, even if you're the best 3-D graphics programmer in the world, unless someone knows about it, it's much more difficult to get hired. So, don't be afraid to meet new people and show off the skills you have. I promise it will eventually be worth it.

The final concept I'll touch on is accessibility. The gaming industry becomes more and more accessible to all of us every day—even across financial boundaries. Consider these options:

- **Game Engines**: The two most popular, Unreal Engine 4 and Unity, are free and open-source (unless you make over $100,000 in profit).

- **Animation and Modeling**: Software like Blender and Maya are free (Maya is free for students only).
- **Art**: Generally either free or low-cost. A monthly license for Adobe costs approximately $29.99/month, but many free alternatives exist: GIMP, Inkscape, and Pixlr, just to name a few. Aseprite is my favorite pixel-art centric art editor for a one-time fee of $15.
- **Music**: Generally either free or low-cost. While industry giants like FL Studio cost you a $99.99 to $899.99 for a one-time purchase, there are plenty of free alternatives like Tracktion 5 or Audacity.
- **Code Editors**: The industry standards, such as Microsoft Visual Studio Code, Sublime Text 3, or Atom, are free.
- **Coworking**: Code-sharing websites like GitHub, the industry standard (and free), are useful for sharing projects with teammates.

The game industry is always evolving, which is a good thing, as it's moving towards a more accessible environment. This might mean the software we use is constantly updating and changing, much to our chagrin. But perhaps that's not such a bad thing when you realize that the software makers are trying to make their programs easier to use, and therefore more accessible, for everyone. That means more and more inspired game-makers, both young and old, can create what they want.

Be ambitious; don't back down from an idea because it's turned down once. People laughed when Satoru Iwata pitched the Nintendo DS, which went on to be the second best-selling gaming device of all time.[346]

Be passionate about what you do. Feargus Urquhart reminds himself to play video games because he loves them, even if he's the CEO of a multimillion-dollar company.

Be smart about what you do. Know your boundaries and what you're willing to sacrifice for those ambitions and passions. Are you okay being isolated from most of humanity, including friends, family, and even loved ones, like Eric Barone found himself doing? Are you okay with the idea of spending years on a failure of a game, or reaching millionaire-level success and fame?

In economics, there's the concept of opportunity cost. It's defined as the cost of the option you're willing to give up when given two. While understanding opportunity cost is fundamental to any two choices in life, it's vital when choosing a career in video games.

Know the opportunity cost of making the choice you want, and may you develop a game that brings you joy and success.

---

346 "Lifetime Global Unit Sales of Video Game Consoles As of September 2020," Statista, accessed October 1, 2020.

APPENDIX

INTRODUCTION

Brunet, Marc. Twitter Post. June 8, 2020. 1:30 a.m. https://twitter.com/bluefley/status/1269864310328537088.

Entertainment Software Association. "U.S. Video Game Sales Reach Record-Breaking $43.4 Billion in 2018." Accessed August 18, 2020. https://www.theesa.com/press-releases/u-s-video-game-sales-reach-record-breaking-43-4-billion-in-2018/.

IBISWorld. "Movie & Video Production Industry in the US - Market Research Report." July 14, 2020. https://www.ibisworld.com/united-states/market-research-reports/movie-video-production-industry/.

Sanusi, Anisa. Twitter Post. June 7, 2020. 4:29 p.m. https://twitter.com/studioanisa/status/1269728164927995908.

Vizcarra, Roxie. Twitter Post. June 10, 2020. 1:48 p.m. https://twitter.com/roxination/status/1270774789687447554.

CHAPTER 1: DAVID CAGE

BAFTA. "2011 Winners & Nominees." British Academy of Film and Television Arts. February 15, 2011. http://www.bafta.org/games/awards/2011-winners-nominees.

Gibson, Ellie. "Quantic Dream Considers Omikron II." Eurogamer, Gamer Network Limited. March 17, 2005. https://www.eurogamer.net/articles/news1703050mikron2.

Glover, Chris. "Eidos Celebrates with Lara Croft Tomb Raider: Anniversary." Sci Entertainment Group. March 11, 2006. Distributed by the Internet Archive Wayback Machine. https://web.archive.org/web/20070810231553/http://corporate.sci.co.uk/Press_Releases/PressReleasesDetail.aspx?Press_Release_ID=228.

Hinkle, David. "Beyond: Two Souls sales topped 1 million in 2013." Engadget, January 10, 2014. https://www.engadget.com/2014-01-10-beyond-two-souls-sales-topped-1-million-in-2013.html.

IGN Entertainment. "Best Adventure Game - Indigo Prophecy." Best of IGN. Accessed August 19, 2020. Distributed by The Internet Archive Wayback Machine. https://web.archive.org/web/20060126205515/http://bestof.ign.com/2005/pc/2.html.

Nelva, Giuseppe. "Quantic Dream's David Cage Talks About His Games, His Career and the PS4: It Allows to 'Go Even Further.'" DualSHOCKERS, January 4, 2015. https://www.dualshockers.com/quantic-dreams-david-cage-talks-about-his-career-and-the-ps4-it-allows-to-go-even-further/.

Pavey, Alex. "Heavy Rain Hits 1 Million Sales." PlayStation Blog,
April 13, 2010. https://blog.playstation.com/archive/2010/04/13/
heavy-rain-hits-1-million-sales/.

Quantic Dream. "Heavy Rain Awarded during the Japan Games
Awards." September 18, 2010. Distributed by The Internet Archive Wayback Machine. https://web.archive.org/
web/20110518014704/http://www.quanticdream.com/fr/news/
heavy-rain-recompense-lors-des-japan-games-awards.

Riaz, Adnan. "David Cage: 'We're Working on Something Very
Exciting.'" GamerHeadlines, November 28, 2014. Distributed by The Internet Archive Wayback Machine. https://web.
archive.org/web/20170628150039/http://www.gamerheadlines.
com/2014/11/david-cage-working-something-exciting/.

Sharkey, Mike. "Heavy Rain Passes the Million Sales Marker."
GameSpy, April 13, 2010. http://ps3.gamespy.com/playstation-3/
quantic-dream-project/1083359p1.html.

Sony Computer Entertainment Inc. "Cumulative Production
Shipments of Hardware (Until March 2007)." Accessed
August 19, 2020. Distributed by The Internet Archive Wayback
Machine. https://web.archive.org/web/20110524023857/http://
www.scei.co.jp/corporate/data/bizdataps_e.html.

Takahashi, Dean. "Why Netease and Quantic Dream Are Teaming
up for Games on Multiple Platforms." VentureBeat, January
29, 2019. https://venturebeat.com/2019/01/29/why-netease-and-
quantic-dream-are-teaming-up-for-games-on-multiple-plat-
forms/view-all/.

CHAPTER 2: HIDETAKA MIYAZAKI

Bishop, Sam. "Demon's Souls Review." IGN, May 9, 2012. https://www.ign.com/articles/2009/10/08/demons-souls-review.

Des Barres, Nick. "Japan Review Check: Demon's Souls." 1Up, January 28, 2019. https://arquivo.pt/wayback/20160522222951/http://www.1up.com/news/japan-review-check-demon-souls.

Famitsu. "Armored Core 4 Review." Kadokawa Game Linkage Inc. Accessed August 21, 2020. https://www.famitsu.com/games/t/960/reviews/.

FromSoftware. "Press Release - New Action Rpg 'Elden Ring' Announced." Accessed August 21, 2020. https://www.fromsoftware.jp/ww/pressrelease_detail.html?tgt=20190610_eldenring_debut.

GigaZine. "ゲーム制作未経験から世界的ヒット作「ダークソウル」を生んだ宮崎英高氏にインタビュー [From Inexperienced Game Developer to Worldwide Bestseller 'Dark Souls': An Interview with Hidetaka Miyazaki]." February 28, 2012. https://gigazine.net/news/20120228-darksouls-miyazaki-interview/.

Japan Game Charts. "Japanese Total Sales from 11 November 2006 to 19 July 2009." Famitsu, August 9, 2009. Distributed by The Internet Archive Wayback Machine. https://web.archive.org/web/20090831085027/http://www.japan-gamecharts.com:80/ps3.php.

Japan Game Charts. "Japanese Total Sales from 11 November 2006 to 19 July 2009." Famitsu, August 9, 2009. Distributed by The Internet Archive Wayback Machine. https://web.archive.org/

web/20090831085027/http://www.japan-gamecharts.com:80/
ps3.php.

Kajita, Mafia. "なぜいまマゾゲーなの？ ゲーマーの間で評判
の"即死ゲー"「Demon's Souls」（デモンズソウル）開発者
インタビュー [Why a Masochistic Game Now? Interview
with 'Demon's Souls' 'Sudden Death Game' Popular among
Gamers]." 4gamer, March 19, 2013. https://www.4gamer.net/
games/080/G008001/20090319002/.

Kim, Matt. "Demon's Souls' Online Service Transformed Its
Multiplayer Into a Literal Ghost Story." USG, November 27,
2017. https://www.usgamer.net/articles/demons-souls-online-
service-was-a-masterpiece.

Kollar, Phil. "Demon's Souls Director Discusses Difficulty, Sequels,
and More." Game Informer, November 5, 2009. https://
www.gameinformer.com/games/demons_souls/b/ps3/
archive/2009/11/05/feature-demon-s-souls-director-discuss-
es-difficulty-sequels-and-more.aspx.

Krabbe, Esra. "Elden Ring Is an Evolution of Dark Souls Says
Creator – E3 2019." IGN, June 21, 2019. https://www.ign.com/
articles/2019/06/21/elden-ring-is-an-evolution-of-dark-souls-
says-creator-a-e3-2019?sf104471595=1.

MacDonald, Keza. "Souls Survivor." *Eurogamer*, May 28,
2010. https://www.eurogamer.net/articles/souls-survivor.

MacDonald, Keza. "The Mind Behind Dark Souls." IGN, January
12, 2018. https://www.ign.com/articles/2011/11/08/the-mind-
behind-dark-souls.

MacDonald, Keza. "Tough Love: On Dark Souls' Difficulty." *Eurogamer*, December 7, 2019. https://www.eurogamer.net/articles/2019-12-07-tough-love-on-dark-souls-difficulty.

MobyGames. "Armored Core 4." Blue Flame Labs. Accessed August 21, 2020. https://www.mobygames.com/game/armored-core-4.

Parkin, Simon. "Bloodborne Creator Hidetaka Miyazaki: 'I Didn't Have a Dream. I Wasn't Ambitious.'" *The Guardian*, March 31, 2015. https://www.theguardian.com/technology/2015/mar/31/bloodborne-dark-souls-creator-hidetaka-miyazaki-interview.

Reilly, Jim. "Sony Talks the Last Guardian, Demon's Souls, and the Vita Launch." Game Informer, February 10, 2012. https://www.gameinformer.com/b/news/archive/2012/02/10/shuhei-yoshida-interview.aspx.

Remo, Chris. "Demon's Souls Sales Triple Atlus Expectations." Gamasutra, April 14, 2010. https://www.gamasutra.com/view/news/119041/Demons_Souls_Sales_Triple_Atlus_Expectations.php.

Remo, Chris. "Sony Regrets Not Publishing Demon's Souls in North America." Gamasutra, March 16, 2010. https://www.gamasutra.com/view/news/27690/Sony_Regrets_Not_Publishing_Demons_Souls_In_North_America.php.

Silliconera. "Demon's Souls Sells Triple What Atlus USA Expected." April 14, 2010. https://www.silliconera.com/demons-souls-sells-triple-what-atlus-usa-expected/.

Sliva, Marty. "Inside the Mind of Bloodborne and Dark Souls' Creator - IGN First." IGN, January 12, 2018. https://www.ign.com/articles/2015/02/05/inside-the-mind-of-bloodborne-and-dark-souls-creator-ign-first.

Tanaka, John. "Tales of the World Remains at Top in Japan." IGN, June 15, 2012. https://www.ign.com/articles/2009/02/13/tales-of-the-world-remains-at-top-in-japan.

Vore, Bryan. "Core Mech Values." Game Informer, Game Informer Magazine. Accessed August 21, 2020. https://web.archive.org/web/20080125123651/http://www.gameinformer.com/NR/exeres/8648C16C-2894-4376-B12E-61F5734DF043.htm.

Dodson, Joe. "Beowulf: The Game Review." GameSpot, November 21, 2007. https://www.gamespot.com/reviews/beowulf-the-game-review/1900-6183284/.

CHAPTER 3: GORDON WALTON

Bolingbroke, Chester. "Game 86: Dungeon of Death (1979)." CRPG Addict (blog), February 7, 2013. https://crpgaddict.blogspot.com/2013/02/game-86-dungeon-of-death-1979.html.

Gamedevthings. "Warren Spector Lecture 11 - Gordon Walton." October 4, 2011. Video, 2:44:21. https://www.youtube.com/watch?v=_UWjsJhp3Sc.

Gunther, Marc. "The Newest Addiction Sony, Sega, Microsoft, and Electronic Arts Are Betting That Games Played over the Internet Will Be the Biggest Thing since Monopoly." CNN

Money, August 2, 1999. https://money.cnn.com/magazines/
fortune/fortune_archive/1999/08/02/263639/index.htm.

Kosak, Dave. "Ten Reasons You Don't Want to Run a Massively
Multiplayer Online Game." GameSpy, March 7, 2003. Distributed by The Internet Archive Wayback Machine. https://web.
archive.org/web/20050301102419/http://archive.gamespy.com/
gdc2003/top10mmog/index.shtml.

Nguyen, Lisa. "15 Shocking Things You Didn't Know about the Miserable Sims Online." The Gamer, September 24, 2017. https://
www.thegamer.com/shocking-things-you-didnt-know-about-
the-miserable-sims-online/.

Old-Games. "Sub Battle Simulator Download (1987 Simulation
Game)." Accessed September 21, 2020. https://www.old-games.
com/download/4445/sub-battle-simulator.

PC Gamer Online. "UbiSoft's Tonic Trouble." Imagine Publishing.
November 10, 1997. Distributed by The Internet Archive Wayback Machine. https://web.archive.org/web/19980218070412/
http://www.pcgamer.com/news/news-1997-11-10.html.

CHAPTER 4: FEARGUS URQUHART

Computer Gaming World Museum. "The Top Ten Games." Computer Gaming World 67, no. 67 (1990): 44. Distributed by The
Internet Archive Wayback Machine. https://web.archive.org/
web/20131205140301/http://www.cgwmuseum.org/galleries/
issues/cgw_67.pdf.

Desslock's RPG News Archives. "Desslock's Ramblings — RPG Sales Figures." GameSpot, May 11, 2000. Distributed by The Internet Archive Wayback Machine. https://web.archive.org/web/20010203124200/http://desslock.gamespot.com/archives/200005/20000511.html.

Digital Dragons. "DD 2016 - Feargus Urquhart: 25 Years Down, 25 Years to Go: A Life Creating Games." June 1 2016. Video, 48:13. https://www.youtube.com/watch?v=UWzY0Vh3CSg.

GamerX. "October's Best-Sellers," CNet Game Center, November 26, 1997. Distributed by The Internet Archive Wayback Machine. https://web.archive.org/web/19990210083600/http://www.gamecenter.com/News/Item/0,3,1331,00.html.

Huffstutter, P.J. "Investment in Interplay." *Los Angeles Times*, May 13, 1999. https://www.latimes.com/archives/la-xpm-1999-may-13-fi-36684-story.html.

IGN. "Legendary RPG Developer Feargus Urquhart - IGN Unfiltered 15." January 31, 2017. Video, 1:07:03. https://www.youtube.com/watch?v=GNMQVcyowss.

Interplay Entertainment Corp. 1992. "Mario Teaches Typing." Accessed August 30, 2020. Distributed by Archive.org. https://archive.org/details/msdos_Mario_Teaches_Typing_1992.

Morris, Daniel. 'Fallout 2.'" GamePro. January 1, 2000. Distributed by The Internet Archive Wayback Machine. https://web.archive.org/web/20081005093851/http://www.gamepro.com/article/reviews/798/fallout2/.

RPGCodex. "RPG Codex Report: A Codexian Visit to inXile Entertainment." InXile Entertainment. April 13, 2017. https://rpgcodex.net//content.php?id=10604.

CHAPTER 5: SATORU IWATA

Andersen, John. "A Former Mentor Recalls the Early Career of Satoru Iwata." Gamasutra, October 9, 2015. https://www.webcitation.org/6cD2alRSz?url=http://www.gamasutra.com/view/news/254169/A_former_mentor_recalls_the_early_career_of_Satoru_Iwata.php.

Crecente, Brian. "Thousands Attend Iwata's Funeral in Kyoto." Polygon. July 17, 2015. https://www.polygon.com/2015/7/17/8988549/thousands-attend-iwatas-funeral-in-kyoto.

Crimmins, Brian. "Why Does HAL Laboratory Only Make Nintendo Games?" *Vice News.* November 21, 2017. Distributed by the Internet Wayback Machine. https://web.archive.org/web/20180902223438if_/https://waypoint.vice.com/en_us/article/ne3mjd/hal-laboratory-metal-slader-glory-nintendo-history

Crossley, Rob. "Nintendo's Iwata Addresses Concerns over Rapid Weight Loss." GameSpot, November 6, 2014. https://www.gamespot.com/articles/nintendos-iwata-addresses-concerns-over-rapid-weig/1100-6423401/.

Davis, Justin. "11 Memorable Satoru Iwata Quotes." IGN Entertainment, July 13, 2015. https://www.ign.com/articles/2015/07/13/11-memorable-satoru-iwata-quotes.

Eurogamer. "Super Smash Bros. - Mii Character Announce Trailer - E3 2014 - Eurogamer." June 10, 2014. Video, 2:18. https://www.youtube.com/watch?v=YdDYoCU2kvo.

GDC. "Satoru Iwata - Heart of a Gamer." July 14, 2015. Video, 1:00:22. https://www.youtube.com/watch?time_continue=11&v=RMrj8gdUfCU&feature=emb_logo.

Hewlett-Packard Development Company, L.P. "HP-65 Programmable Pocket Calculator, 1974." Accessed August 30, 2020. http://www.hp.com/hpinfo/abouthp/histnfacts/museum/personalsystems/0024/index.html.

IGN Entertainment. "Profile: Satoru Iwata." Last updated June 17, 2012. https://www.ign.com/articles/2004/07/16/profile-satoru-iwata.

Inoue, Osamu. *Nintendo Magic: Winning the Videogame Wars.* New York: Vertical, Inc., 2010.

Inoue, Osamu. "Iwata and Miyamoto: Business Ascetics - an Excerpt from Nintendo Magic." Gamasutra, May 14, 2010. https://www.gamasutra.com/view/feature/4418/iwata_and_miyamoto_business_.php?page=3.

Investor Relation Information. "Dedicated Video Game Sales Units." Nintendo. June 30, 2020. https://www.nintendo.co.jp/ir/en/finance/hard_soft/index.html.

Iwata Asks. "Just Being President Was a Waste!" Nintendo. Accessed August 30, 2020. http://iwataasks.nintendo.com/interviews/#/ds/pokemon/0/2.

Kosak, Dave. "Game Developers Rant!" GameSpy, March 16, 2005. http://www.gamespy.com/articles/596/596734p1.html.

Kreps, Daniel. "Satoru Iwata, President and CEO of Nintendo, Dead at 55." *Rolling Stone*, July 13, 2015. https://www.rollingstone.com/culture/culture-news/satoru-iwata-president-and-ceo-of-nintendo-dead-at-55-187158/.

Makuch, Eddie. "Nintendo President Not Coming to E3 on Doctor's Advice." GameSpot, June 8, 2014. https://www.gamespot.com/articles/nintendo-president-not-coming-to-e3-on-doctors-advice/1100-6420132/.

Mainichi Interactive. "キーマンインタビュー→任天堂社長岩田聡さん：新ハードでびっくりさせる [Key Interview with Nintendo President Satoru Iwata: Surprise Them with New Hardware]." Accessed August 30, 2020. Distributed by The Internet Archive Wayback Machine. https://web.archive.org/web/20040401145640/https://www.mainichi.co.jp/life/hobby/game/interview/34.html.

Moriarty, Colin. "Sony's Documentary on PlayStation 2's Retail Dominance." IGN Entertainment, February 16, 2013. https://www.ign.com/articles/2013/02/17/sonys-documentary-on-playstation-2s-retail-dominance.

Nakamura, Toshi. "Smash Bros. Creator Remembers Satoru Iwata." Kotaku, July 22, 2015. https://kotaku.com/smash-bros-creator-remembers-satoru-iwata-1719451777.

Nintendo Co., Ltd. "Consolidated Sales Transition by Region." Accessed August 30, 2020. Distributed by The Inter-

net Archive Wayback Machine. https://web.archive.org/
web/20111027052007/http://www.nintendo.co.jp/ir/library/
historical_data/pdf/consolidated_sales_e1106.pdf.

Nintendo Co., Ltd. "Notification of Death and Personnel Change
of a Representative Director (President)." July 13, 2015. https://
www.nintendo.co.jp/ir/pdf/2015/150713e.pdf.

Nintendo. Twitter post. June 12, 2015. https://twitter.com/Nin-
tendo/status/609514061475115008.

Peckham, Matt. "Why Nintendo President Satoru Iwata Mattered."
Time, July 13, 2015. https://time.com/3954934/nintendo-sato-
ru-iwata/.

PlayStation. Twitter post. July 12, 2015. https://twitter.com/Play-
Station/status/620412765849546752.

Plunkett, Luke. "The Video Game Community Pays Tribute To Satoru Iwata." Kotaku, July 12, 2015. https://kotaku.
com/the-video-game-community-pays-tribute-to-satoru-
iwata-1717397315.

Reimer, Jeremy. "Nintendo Boss Levels up to 'Top 30 CEO'." Ars
Technica, March 28, 2007. https://arstechnica.com/gam-
ing/2007/03/nintendo-boss-levels-up-to-top-30-ceo/.

Robinson, Martin. "Satoru Iwata: A Gentle Revolutionary."
Eurogamer, July 14, 2015. https://www.eurogamer.net/arti-
cles/2015-07-13-it-would-have-been-more-frightening-to-take-
the-conventional-path-remembering-iwata.

Sarkar, Samit. "A Visit to the Satoru Iwata Memorial at New York's Nintendo World Store." Polygon, July 13, 2015. https://www.polygon.com/2015/7/13/8954863/satoru-iwata-memorial-nintendo-world-store.

Stack, Liam. "Satoru Iwata, Nintendo Chief Executive, Dies at 55." *The New York Times*, July 13, 2015. https://www.nytimes.com/2015/07/13/business/satoru-iwata-nintendo-chief-executive-dies-at-55.html.

Statista. "Lifetime Global Unit Sales of Video Game Consoles As of September 2020." Accessed October 1, 2020. https://www.statista.com/statistics/268966/total-number-of-game-consoles-sold-worldwide-by-console-type/.

Used Games Magazine. "Satoru Iwata - 1999 Developer Interview." Accessed August 30, 2020. Distributed by Shmuplations. http://shmuplations.com/iwata/.

Williams, Mike. "Teens React to Mega Man: What We've Forgotten about 'Nintendo Hard' Games." USGamer, December 15, 2014. https://www.usgamer.net/articles/teens-react-to-mega-man-what-we-forget-about-nintendo-hard-games.

CHAPTER 6: REGGIE FILS-AIMÉ

Aguirre A., Francisco. "Reggie Fils-Aimé, Presidente de Nintendo América: "Nos Dolió que los Fanáticos No Entendieran a Wii U [Reggie Fils-Aimé, President of Nintendo of America: It Hurt Us That Fans Didn't Understand Wii U]," *La Tercera*, June 20, 2016. https://www.latercera.com/noticia/

reggie-Fils-Aimé-presidente-de-nintendo-america-nos-dol-
io-que-los-fanaticos-no-entendieran-a-wii-u/.

Hall, Kenji. "The Big Ideas Behind Nintendo's Wii." BusinessWeek,
November 16, 2006. Distributed by The Internet Archive Wayback Machine. https://web.archive.org/web/20061201013947/
http://www.businessweek.com/technology/content/nov2006/
tc20061116_750580.htm.

Cornell SC Johnson College of Business. "Reggie Fils-Aimé '83
- Principle 6: Courage In Decision-Making." October 30,
2019. Video, 2:15. https://www.youtube.com/watch?v=FbK_
z5fnc48&list=PLlE53j2qAnJfLAqvB_npPlknzWf2EY-QY&in-
dex=6.

Syed Islam. "Reggie Fils-Aimé on Wii Sports." October 22, 2019.
Video, 1:01. https://www.youtube.com/watch?v=P-G3dNgjLtI.

E3 2006. "Outline of Wii." Nintendo co. Accessed August 31,
2020. Distributed by The Internet Archive Wayback Machine.
https://web.archive.org/web/20060706011413/http://www.nin-
tendo.co.jp/n10/e3_2006/wii/controller.html.

Gadgetress. "Wii BMI Test." July 16, 2007. Video, 5:11. https://www.
youtube.com/watch?v=PvdM9I_tTtQ.

Guinness World Rec Gamers Ed. London: Little Brown Books, 2008,
Digital. Distributed by Archive.org. https://archive.org/details/
guinnessworldrecooguin_0/page/50/mode/2up.

Investor Relations Information. "Dedicated Video Game Sales Units." Nintendo. June 30, 2020. https://www.nintendo.co.jp/ir/en/finance/hard_soft/index.html.

Kohler, Chris. "How Reggie Fils-Aimé Became a Nintendo Legend." Kotaku, February 22, 2019. https://kotaku.com/how-reggie-Fils-Aimé-became-a-nintendo-legend-1832817677.

Machkovech, Sam. "The Story of How Nintendo's Iconic Logo Escaped an 'Age-Up' Remake." Ars Technica, January 27, 2020. https://arstechnica.com/gaming/2020/01/the-story-of-how-nintendos-iconic-logo-escaped-an-age-up-remake/.

McFerran, Damien. "Wii U's Failure Is Responsible for Switch's Success, Says Reggie." Nintendo Life, November 10, 2016. https://www.nintendolife.com/news/2017/11/wii_us_failure_is_responsible_for_switchs_success_says_reggie.

Mudhar, Raju. "E3 Interview With Nintendo's Reggie Fils-Aimé: What's So Special About Canadian Videogamers?" *The Star,* June 15, 2018. https://www.thestar.com/entertainment/gaming/2018/06/15/e3-interview-nintendo-super-smashes-expectations-with-switch.html.

Nintendo. "First Look at Nintendo Switch." October 20, 2016. Video, 3:37. https://youtu.be/f5uik5fgIaI.

Nintendo. "Nintendo Digital Event." September 14, 2015. Video, 48:25. https://www.youtube.com/watch?v=C73f618-3pk.

Nintendo. "Reggie Fils-Aimé Full Speech (Super Smash Bros. Invitational 2014)." June 11, 2014. Video, 6:21. https://www.youtube.com/watch?v=q8dflFZ3aqs.

Nintendo. "Reggie Fils-A-Mech - Announcing Nintendo @ E3 2014." April 29, 2014. Video, 5:02. https://www.youtube.com/watch?v=ghEhI4CJjAM.

Nintendo Co., Ltd. "Annual Report 2015." Accessed August 31, 2020. https://www.nintendo.co.jp/ir/pdf/2015/annual1503e.pdf.

NintendoPro. "Nintendo E3 2004 Press Conference (Event) - Part 1 of 4." April 13, 2011. Video, 15:00. https://www.youtube.com/watch?v=89GB6bC9_N4.

Peckham, Matt. "Nintendo 3DS Sells 400,000 in Japan, Already R4 Hacked." PCWorld, February 28, 2011. https://www.pcworld.com/article/220875/nintendo_3ds_sells_400000_in_japan_aready_r4_hacked.html.

Peterson, Kim. "Putting Nintendo Back in the Game." *The Seattle Times,* November 12, 2006. https://www.seattletimes.com/business/putting-nintendo-back-in-the-game/.

Planet3DS. "Nintendo 3DS: Reggie Fils-Aimé Interviewed on MSNBC." January 6, 2011. Video, 2:32. https://www.youtube.com/watch?v=Ai_FqoWrIP4.

PlayscopeTimeline. "The Legend of Zelda - Twilight Princess - Trailer E3 2004 - GameCube.mov." December 27, 2009. Video. 1:05. https://www.youtube.com/watch?v=RieKG7pw6g8.

Priestman, Chris. "Reggie Fils-Aimé Prevented Nintendo from Having a Graffiti Logo." IGN Entertainment, January 27, 2020. https://in.ign.com/reggiefilsaime/144160/news/reggie-Fils-Aimé-prevented-nintendo-from-having-a-graffiti-logo.

Fils-Aimé, Reggie. "Life As the Regginator." Interview by Bobbi Dempsey. *The New York Times*, November 18, 2007. https://www.nytimes.com/2007/11/18/jobs/18boss.html.

Sinclair, Brendan. "3DS Amazon UK's Most Preordered System Ever." GameSpot, March 17, 2011. Distributed by The Internet Archive Wayback Machine. https://web.archive.org/web/20110321015218/http://www.gamespot.com/news/6304525.html.

Souppouris, Aaron. "'Switch' is Nintendo's Next Game Console." Engadget, October 20, 2016. https://www.engadget.com/2016-10-20-switch-is-nintendos-next-game-console.html.

StevoniStuffThings. "The Very Bad Wii U Ads." July 6, 2017. Video, 6:47. https://youtu.be/SChWdprUnzw.

Syed Islam. "Reggie Fils-Aimé on Memes in Marketing." October 22, 2019. Video, 2:16. https://www.youtube.com/watch?v=p4_JdO35cgM.

The Tonight Show Starring Jimmy Fallon. "Jimmy Fallon Debuts the Nintendo Switch." December 7, 2016. Video, 9:40. https://youtu.be/7TJ7IUNWGl4.

Yin-Poole, Wesley. "Nintendo NX Is 'New Hardware with a Brand New Concept'." *Eurogamer*, June 5, 2015. https://www.eurogamer.net/articles/2015-03-17-nintendo-nx-is-new-hardware-with-a-brand-new-concept.

CHAPTER 7: SHIGERU MIYAMOTO

Borow, Zev. "Why Nintendo Won't Grow Up." *Wired,* January 1, 2003. https://www.wired.com/2003/01/nintendo-4/.

Futter, Mike. "Shigeru Miyamoto Discusses His Favorite Movie and Games of 2015." Game Informer, March 4, 2016. https://www.gameinformer.com/b/news/archive/2016/03/04/shigeru-miyamoto-discusses-his-favorite-movie-and-games-of-2015.aspx.

Gordon, Nakia S., Sara Kollack-Walker, Huda Akil, and Jaak Panksepp. "Expression of C-Fos Gene Activation during Rough and Tumble Play in Juvenile Rats." PubMed. National Center for Biotechnology Information, March 2002. https://pubmed.ncbi.nlm.nih.gov/11927369/.

Jones, Robert Snowdon. "Home Video Games Are Coming under a Strong Attack." *Cox News Service,* December 12, 1982. https://news.google.com/newspapers?nid=1320&-dat=19821212&id=L2tWAAAAIBAJ&sjid=q-kDAAAAIBA-J&pg=1609,4274079&hl=en.

Moss, Stephen. "Natural Childhood Report." National Trust of the United Kingdom. Accessed August 25, 2020. https://nt.global.ssl.fastly.net/documents/read-our-natural-childhood-report.pdf.

Nakamura, Yuji. "Peak Video Game? Top Analyst Sees Industry Slumping in 2019." *Bloomberg News,* January 23, 2019. https://

www.bloomberg.com/news/articles/2019-01-23/peak-video-game-top-analyst-sees-industry-slumping-in-2019.

Nix, Marc. "IGN Presents: The History of Super Mario Bros." IGN Entertainment, September 17, 2015. https://www.ign.com/articles/2010/09/14/ign-presents-the-history-of-super-mario-bros.

O'Kane, Sean. "7 Things I Learned from the Designer of the NES." *The Verge,* October 18, 2015. https://www.theverge.com/2015/10/18/9554885/nintendo-entertainment-system-famicom-history-masayuki-uemura.

Paumgarten, Nick. "Master of Play." *The New Yorker,* December 13, 2010. https://www.newyorker.com/magazine/2010/12/20/master-of-play.

Schiesel, Seth. "Resistance Is Futile." *The New York Times,* May 25, 2008. https://www.nytimes.com/2008/05/25/arts/television/25schi.html.

Stuart, Keith. "Super Mario Bros: 25 Mario Facts for the 25th Anniversary." *The Guardian,* September 13, 2010. Distributed by The Internet Archive Wayback Machine. https://web.archive.org/web/20170825023929/https://amp.theguardian.com/technology/gamesblog/2010/sep/13/games-gameculture.

CHAPTER 8: INGRID SANASSEE

Dodson, Joe. "Beowulf: The Game Review." GameSpot, CBS Interactive Inc. November 21, 2007. https://www.gamespot.com/reviews/beowulf-the-game-review/1900-6183284/.

Iwaniuk, Phil. "Beyond: Two Souls Review – an Essential Purchase for Interactive-Drama Fans." Official PlayStation Magazine UK, October 8, 2013. Distributed by The Internet Archive Wayback Machine. https://web.archive.org/web/20131009132059/http://www.officialplaystationmagazine.co.uk/review/beyond-two-souls-review-official-playstation-magazine/.

McElroy, Justin. "Beyond Two Souls Review: Hand in Hand." Polygon, October 8, 2013. Distributed by The Internet Archive Wayback Machine. https://web.archive.org/web/20131008150859/http://www.polygon.com/2013/10/8/4814738/beyond-two-souls-review.

Quantic Dream. "Quantic Dream & Me - Interview with Ingrid, Motion Kit Lead." October 31, 2019. https://blog.quanticdream.com/quantic-dream-me-interview-with-ingrid-motion-kit-lead/.

Quantic Dream. "Temps fort : Inaugural Quantic Dream Livestream." May 25, 2020. Video. 2:47:51. https://www.twitch.tv/videos/631930354.

Steam Spy. "I Am Alive." Steam. Accessed August 24, 2020. https://steamspy.com/app/214250.

The World Bank Group. "GDP Per Capita (Constant 2010 US$) - Mauritius." Accessed September 16, 2019. https://data.worldbank.org/indicator/NY.GDP.PCAP.KD?locations=MU

CHAPTER 9: AMY HENNIG

Barker, Sammy. "People Ask for Story-Based Games, but Don't Necessarily Buy Them." Push Square, January 22, 2018. https://www.pushsquare.com/news/2018/01/people_ask_for_story-based_games_but_dont_necessarily_buy_them.

Crecente, Brian. "Silicon Knights: Epic Sabotaged Us." Kotaku. G/O Media. July 19, 2007. Distributed by The Internet Archive Wayback Machine. https://web.archive.org/web/20090916170528/http://kotaku.com/280491/silicon-knights-epic-sabotaged-us.

Fritz, Ben. "How I Made It: Amy Hennig." Los Angeles Times, February 7, 2010. https://www.latimes.com/archives/la-xpm-2010-feb-07-la-fi-himi7-2010feb07-story.html.

IGN Entertainment. "Best of 2007." Accessed August 25, 2020. https://www.webcitation.org/6600QYSI7?url=http://bestof.ign.com/2007/.

IGN Entertainment. "Uncharted PS4 Writer Amy Hennig Leaves Naughty Dog." June 24, 2020. https://www.ign.com/articles/2014/03/05/uncharted-ps4-writer-amy-hennig-leaves-naughty-dog?abthid=5316b21a733900a265000049.

LinkedIn Corporation. "Amy Hennig." Accessed August 25, 2020. https://www.linkedin.com/in/amy-hennig-1385851/

MBMMaverick. "Seriously? I Paid $80 To Have Vader Locked?" Reddit Post. Accessed September 17, 2020. https://www.reddit.com/r/StarWarsBattlefront/comments/7cffob/seriously_i_paid_80_to_have_vader_locked/dppum98/.

McWhertor, Michael. "Amy Hennig's New Studio Will Make 'Story-Focused' Games for 'Emerging Streaming Platforms'." Polygon, November 18, 2019. https://www.polygon.com/2019/11/18/20971213/amy-hennig-skydance-media-streaming-games.

Metacritic. "Uncharted 2: Among Thieves." October 13, 2009. https://www.metacritic.com/game/playstation-3/uncharted-2-among-thieves.

Minotti, Mike. "EA's Defense of Star Wars: Battlefront II is Now Reddit's Most Downvoted Comment." VentureBeat, November 12, 2017. https://venturebeat.com/2017/11/12/eas-defense-of-star-wars-battlefront-ii-is-now-reddits-most-downvoted-comment/.

Nunneley, Stephany. "Epic Judgment Doubled, Silicon Knights Ordered to Pay over $9 Million." VG247, November 9, 2012. Distributed by The Internet Archive Wayback Machine. https://web.archive.org/web/20160808040934/http://www.vg247.com/2012/11/09/epic-judgment-doubled-silicon-knights-ordered-to-pay-over-9-million/.

Phillips, Tom. "Uncharted Creator Amy Hennig Has Departed EA, and Her Star Wars Game Is 'On the Shelf'." Eurogamer, June 28, 2018. https://www.eurogamer.net/articles/2018-06-28-uncharted-creator-amy-hennig-has-departed-ea-to-set-up-indie-studio.

Purchese, Robert. "Uncharted Sequel to Cost USD 20 Million." Eurogamer, February 5, 2009. https://www.eurogamer.net/articles/uncharted-sequel-costing-usd-20-million.

Rubenstein, Jeff. "Uncharted 3: Drake's Deception Gameplay Reveal." PlayStation Blog, December 17, 2010. https://blog.playstation.com/2010/12/17/uncharted-3-drakes-deception-gameplay-reveal/.

Takahashi, Dean. "Amy Hennig Interview — Surviving the Trauma of Making a Video Game and Inspiring Newcomers." Venture Beat, February 22, 2019. https://venturebeat.com/2019/02/22/amy-hennig-interview-surviving-the-trauma-of-making-a-video-game-and-inspiring-newcomers/2/.

The Sydney Morning Herald. "Dude Raiders." October 4, 2007. Distributed by The Internet Archive Wayback Machine. https://web.archive.org/web/20081006180015/http://www.smh.com.au/news/articles/dude-raiders/2007/10/03/1191091178051.html.

Thomsen, Michael. "Inside the Story: Naughty Dog Interview." IGN, May 12, 2012. https://www.ign.com/articles/2008/02/05/inside-the-story-naughty-dog-interview.

Thorsen, Tor. "PS3 Motion Controller Revealed, God of War III Due in March." GameSpot, June 2, 2009. Distributed by The Internet Archive Wayback Machine. https://web.archive.org/web/20120217043755/http://e3.gamespot.com/story/6210509/ps3-motion-controller-revealed-god-of-war-iii-due-in-march.

Wells, Evan. "Uncharted 2 Takes Game of the Year at VGAs — behind the Scenes with Naughty Dog's Evan Wells." PlayStation Blog, December 18, 2009. Distributed by The Internet Archive Wayback Machine. https://web.archive.org/web/20190307181401/https://blog.us.playstation.

com/2009/12/18/uncharted-2-takes-game-of-the-year-at-vgas-behind-the-scenes-with-naughty-dogs-evan-wells/.

CHAPTER 10: IAN SCHREIBER

Akins, Jacob. "Video Game Design Colleges | 77 Best Schools for 2020." Successful Student, May 29, 2020. https://successfulstudent.org/best-video-game-colleges/.

Animation Arena. "Video Game Design School." Accessed August 25, 2020. Distributed by The Internet Archive Wayback Machine. https://web.archive.org/web/20050109091823/http://www.animationarena.com/video-game-design-school.html.

Animation Arena. "Video Game Design School." Accessed August 25, 2020. http://www.animationarena.com/video-game-design-school.html.

Lassman, Forest. "How Game Companies Use Credits to Reward, or Punish, Developers." Kotaku, January 9, 2020. https://kotaku.com/how-game-companies-use-credits-to-reward-or-punish-de-1840905129.

Williams, Christina. "Udemy Discounts Courses Up To 95% Off For Flash Sale." New York Post, March 30, 2020. https://nypost.com/2020/03/30/udemy-sale/.

CHAPTER 11: LARRY MELLON

IGN. "The Sims Online." Accessed October 1, 2020. Distributed by The Internet Archive Wayback Machine. https://web.archive.

org/web/20080822012539/http://pc.ign.com/objects/015/015970. html.

Park, Andrew. "The Sims Online Review." GameSpot, December 18, 2002. https://www.gamespot.com/reviews/the-sims-online-review/1900-2908060/.

Terdiman, Daniel. "'EA Land' Closing Just Weeks after Debut." *CNet,* April 29, 2008. Distributed by The Internet Archive Wayback Machine. https://web.archive.org/web/20110617023122/http://news.cnet.com/8301-17938_105-9931757-1.html

CHAPTER 12: ERIC BARONE

Baker, Chris. "The 4 Years of Self-Imposed Crunch That Went into Stardew Valley." Gamasutra, March 9, 2016. https://www.gamasutra.com/view/news/267563/The_4_years_of_selfimposed_crunch_that_went_into_Stardew_Valley.php.

Chalk, Andy. "Stardew Valley Has Sold More Than 10 Million Copies." *PC Gamer,* January 23, 2020. https://www.pcgamer.com/stardew-valley-has-sold-more-than-10-million-copies/.

ConcernedApe. Twitter Post. November 26, 2020, 3:31 p.m. https://twitter.com/ConcernedApe/status/1232765041297874946.

ConcernedApe. Twitter post. November 26, 2019. 2:22 p.m. https://twitter.com/ConcernedApe/status/1199408101499097088.

ConcernedApe. Twitter post. December 20, 2018. 3:37 p.m. http://twitter.com/ConcernedApe/status/1075852647402356736.

Forbes. "Eric Barone." Accessed August 19, 2020. https://www.
forbes.com/profile/eric-barone/#47bd7ada153a.

Hernandez, Patricia. "A Surprising Number of People Feel Bad
for Pirating *Stardew Valley.*" Kotaku, March 2, 2016. https://
kotaku.com/a-surprising-number-of-people-feel-bad-for-pi-
rating-sta-1762379596.

Marks, Tom. "Interview: What's Next for Stardew Valley." PC
Gamer. Future US Inc. March 10, 2016. https://www.pcgamer.
com/stardew-valley-interview/.

PC Gamer. "The Creators of Stardew Valley and Harvest Moon
Talk to Us about Farm Games." December 1, 2016. Video,
16:58. https://www.youtube.com/watch?time_contin-
ue=46&v=ceFR8--6Obo&feature=emb_logo.

Schreier, Jason. *Blood, Sweat, and Pixels: The Triumphant and Turbulent Stories Behind How Video Games are Made.* New York
City: Harper Paperbacks, 2017.

White, Sam. "Valley Forged: How One Man Made the Indie
Video Game Sensation Stardew Valley." *GQ Magazine*, March
20, 2018. https://www.gq.com/story/stardew-valley-eric-bar-
one-profile.

Wijman, Tom. "The Global Games Market Will Generate $152.1 Bil-
lion in 2019 as the U.S. Overtakes China as the Biggest Market."
Newzoo, June 18, 2019. https://newzoo.com/insights/articles/
the-global-games-market-will-generate-152-1-billion-in-2019-
as-the-u-s-overtakes-china-as-the-biggest-market/.

CHAPTER 13: MARKUS PERSSON

Carlyle, Erin. "'Minecraft' Billionaire Markus Persson Buys $70 Million Beverly Hills Contemporary with Car Lift." Forbes. December 18, 2014. https://www.forbes.com/sites/erincarlyle/2014/12/18/minecraft-billionaire-markus-persson-buys-70-million-beverly-hills-contemporary-with-car-lift/#6af8b91d2a3b.

Handy, Alex. "Interview: Markus 'Notch' Persson Talks Making Minecraft." Gamasutra, Informa PLC. March 23, 2010. https://www.gamasutra.com/view/news/27719/Interview_Markus_Notch_Persson_Talks_Making_Minecraft.php.

Java Unlimited. "Java 4K Programming Contest." July 17, 2011. Distributed by The Internet Archive Wayback Machine. https://web.archive.org/web/20110717160452/http://javaunlimited.net/contests/java4k.php.

Mac, Ryan. "Inside The Post-Minecraft Life Of Billionaire Gamer God Markus Persson." *Forbes*, March 3, 2015. https://www.forbes.com/sites/ryanmac/2015/03/03/minecraft-markus-persson-life-after-microsoft-sale/#5f0ef7751616.

Minecraft Wiki. "Java Edition Version History." Gamepedia. Accessed August 20, 2020. https://minecraft.gamepedia.com/Java_Edition_version_history#:~:text=Alpha%20lasted%20from%20June%2030,the%20most%20recent%20being%201.15..

Notch. Twitter Post. August 29, 2015, 5:53a.m. https://twitter.com/notch/status/637563733124980736?ref_src=twsrc%5Etfw%7Ctwcamp%5Etweetembed%7Ctwterm%5E637563733124980736.

Pagliery, Jose. "Microsoft Buys Minecraft for $2.5 billion." CNN Business, Cable News Network. September 15, 2014. https://money.cnn.com/2014/09/15/technology/minecraft-microsoft/.

Parrish, Kevin. "Minecraft Creator Notch Says EA is Destroying Gaming." Tom's Hardware, Future US Inc. May 6, 2012. https://www.tomshardware.com/news/Mojang-Notch-EA-Indie-Minecraft,15546.html.

Paul, Ian. "Microsoft Buys Minecraft Maker Mojang for $2.5 Billion." PCWorld. IDG Communications. September 15, 2014. https://www.pcworld.com/article/2683173/microsoft-buys-minecraft-maker-mojang-for-25-billion.html.

Statista. "Cumulative Number of Copies of Minecraft Sold Worldwide as of May 2020." Accessed September 15, 2020. https://www.statista.com/statistics/680124/minecraft-unit-sales-worldwide/.

The Guardian. "Markus Persson: The Minecraft Billionaire Sending Lonely Late-Night Tweets from Ibiza." Guardian News & Media Limited. September 1, 2015. https://www.theguardian.com/global/shortcuts/2015/sep/01/markus-persson-the-minecraft-billionaire-sending-lonely-late-night-tweets-from-ibiza.

The Word of Notch. "Top Ten Movies of 2011!" Tumblr post. December 31, 2011. https://notch.tumblr.com/post/15078260435/top-ten-movies-of-2011.

CHAPTER 14: JAN RIGERL

Bevan, Lottie. "British Game Dev Salaries." Weather Factory, July 17, 2020. https://weatherfactory.biz/british-game-dev-salaries/.

Dev-M Games. "Desert Worms." February 23, 2017. http://devmgames.com/?page=devlog.

Dev-M Games. "LightmapLightApproximator.cs for Unity." May 29, 2013. http://devmgames.com/?page=devlog&offset=1.

Dev-M Games. "Moving Out." December 12, 2019. http://devmgames.com/?page=devlog.

Dev-M Games. "Unity Font Importer - Devlog." June 6, 2014. http://devmgames.com/?page=devlog&offset=1.

Encyclopaedia Britannica Online. Academic ed. s.v. "Commedia Dell'arte."Accessed August 25, 2020. https://www.britannica.com/art/commedia-dellarte.

GameCentral. "Moving Out Nintendo Switch Review - Couch (and Fridge and TV) Co-op." *Metro*, April 24, 2020. https://metro.co.uk/2020/04/24/moving-nintendo-switch-review-couch-fridge-tv-co-op-12605330/.

Nintendo. "Moving Out - Announcement Trailer - Nintendo Switch." March 17, 2020. Video, 1:35. https://www.youtube.com/watch?v=mlYQoZGogac.

Ogilvie, Tristan. "Moving Out Review." IGN, September 11, 2020. https://www.ign.com/articles/moving-out-review.

PlayStation Blog. "How Playtesting Improved Moving Out, Out on ps4 Tomorrow." Sony Interactive Entertainment. April 27, 2020. https://blog.playstation.com/2020/04/27/how-playtesting-improved-moving-out-out-on-ps4-today/.

SMG Studio. Twitter post. April 30, 2020. https://twitter.com/smg-studio/status/1255904698575405056.

Steam Community. "Moving Out Monday #17 – DevM + SMG." Valve Corporation. May 4, 2020. https://steamcommunity.com/games/996770/announcements/detail/2226411153670478042.

Steam. "Moving Out." Valve Corporation. Accessed August 25, 2020. https://store.steampowered.com/app/996770/Moving_Out/.

Team17. "Moving Out - Reveal Trailer (Nintendo Switch, PC, PS4 and Xbox One)." August 29, 2020. Video, 1:09. https://www.youtube.com/watch?v=7GmIvduEzP8&feature=emb_title.

McDonald, Keza, and Keith Stuart. "The Best Games of 2020 So Far." *The Guardian*, May 15, 2020. https://www.theguardian.com/games/2020/may/15/the-best-games-of-2020-so-far?.

CHAPTER 15: DAKOTA HEROLD

Rosen, Ellen. "RIT Video Game Design Programs Again Ranked Among the Best." Rochester Institute of Technology, March 12, 2019. https://www.rit.edu/news/rit-video-game-design-programs-again-ranked-among-best.

Stack Overflow. "2015 Developer Survey." Accessed August 24, 2020. https://insights.stackoverflow.com/survey/2015.

Stack Overflow. "2019 Developer Survey." Accessed August 24, 2020. https://insights.stackoverflow.com/survey/2019.

CHAPTER 16: TODAY'S VIDEO GAME MARKETING LANDSCAPE

Bärtl, Mathias. "YouTube Channels, Uploads, and Views: A Statistical Analysis of the past 10 Years." Convergence: The International Journal of Research into New Media Technologies. Sage Journals, January 10, 2018. https://journals.sagepub.com/doi/10.1177/1354856517736979.

Carmody, Tim. "It's Not TV, It's the Web: YouTube Partners Complain about Google Ads, Revenue Sharing." The Verge, March 4, 2013. https://www.theverge.com/2013/3/4/4062810/youtube-partners-complain-revenue-sharing-google-ads.

Clement, J. "YouTube: Share of Google Revenues 2017-2019." Statista, February 5, 2020. https://www.statista.com/statistics/289659/youtube-share-of-google-total-ad-revenues/.

Forbes. "GooTube." May 29, 2008. https://www.forbes.com/forbes/2008/0616/050.html.

Gerasimenko, Dmitry. "Investor Money vs. Public Interest: Did Google Fail to Build a Non-evil Platform?" Medium, September 30, 2019. https://medium.com/swlh/investor-money-vs-public-interest-did-google-fail-to-build-a-non-evil-platform-3a054f996ea9.

Google Trends. "Influencer." Google. Accessed September 1, 2020. https://trends.google.com/trends/explore?date=all&-geo=US&q=influencer.

Graham, Jefferson. "Video Websites Pop Up, Invite Postings." *USA Today,* November 21, 2005. https://usatoday30.usatoday.com/tech/news/techinnovations/2005-11-21-video-websites_x.htm.

Kim, Eugene. "Amazon Buys Twitch for $US970 Million in Cash." Business Insider Australia, August 26, 2014. https://www.businessinsider.com.au/amazon-buys-twitch-2014-8.

Perez, Sarah. "Twitch Continues to Dominate Live Streaming with Its Second-Biggest Quarter to Date." Tech Crunch, July 12, 2019. https://techcrunch.com/2019/07/12/twitch-continues-to-dominate-live-streaming-with-its-second-biggest-quarter-to-date/.

Robehmed, Natalie, and Madeline Berg. "Highest-Paid You-Tube Stars 2018: Markiplier, Jake Paul, Pewdiepie and More." *Forbes,* December 3, 2018. https://www.forbes.com/sites/natalierobehmed/2018/12/03/highest-paid-youtube-stars-2018-markiplier-jake-paul-pewdiepie-and-more/.

Spangler, Todd. "YouTube Now Has 2 Billion Monthly Users, Who Watch 250 Million Hours on TV Screens Daily." *Variety,* May 3, 2019. https://variety.com/2019/digital/news/youtube-2-billion-users-tv-screen-watch-time-hours-1203204267/.

Takahashi, Dean. "YouTube Gaming Videos Were Viewed for 50 Billion Hours in 2018." Venture Beat, December 8, 2018. https://

venturebeat.com/2018/12/08/youtube-game-videos-were-viewed-for-50-billion-hours-in-2018/.

Tech Crunch. "YouTube Launches Revenue Sharing Partners Program, but No Pre-rolls." May 4, 2007. https://techcrunch.com/2007/05/04/youtube-launches-revenue-sharing-partners-program-but-no-pre-rolls/.

Wagner, Adam. "Are You Maximizing the Use of Video in Your Content Marketing Strategy?" *Forbes*, May 15, 2017. https://www.forbes.com/sites/forbesagencycouncil/2017/05/15/are-you-maximizing-the-use-of-video-in-your-content-marketing-strategy/.

Wilhelm, Alex. "TwitchTV: Justin.tv's Killer New Esports Project." The Next Web, June 6, 2011. https://thenextweb.com/media/2011/06/06/twitchtv-justin-tvs-killer-new-esports-project/.

Winkler, Rolfe. "YouTube Growing Faster Than Thought, Report Says." *Wall Street Journal,* December 11, 2013. Distributed by The Internet Archive Wayback Machine. https://web.archive.org/web/20200614200237/https://blogs.wsj.com/digits/2013/12/11/streaming-video-means-streaming-dollars-for-youtube/.

YouTube. "YouTube for Press." Google. Accessed September 1, 2020. https://www.youtube.com/intl/en-GB/about/press/.

YouTube. "YouTube Rewind 2019: For the Record | #YouTubeRewind." December 5, 2019. Video, 5:36. https://www.youtube.com/watch?v=2lAe1cqCOXo&feature=youtu.be.

CHAPTER 17: LISA PENDSE

Chang, Lulu. "Gamers are Being Targeted By Energy Drink Companies." Digital Trends, May 20, 2015. https://www.digitaltrends.com/gaming/energy-drinks-target-gamers/.

Derschowitz, Jessica. "Kids' Choice Awards 2013: List of Winners." CBS News, March 23, 2013. https://www.cbsnews.com/news/kids-choice-awards-2013-list-of-winners/.

GameSpot. "Just Dance E3 Opening | Ubisoft E3 2018." June 11, 2018. Video, 4:01. https://www.youtube.com/watch?v=aqfReVKktb8&feature=emb_logo.

Maguid, Youssef. "Women of Ubisoft - Lisa Pendse." Ubisoft, October 26, 2018. https://news.ubisoft.com/en-us/article/3JPESNFr6qgSyFWGnjmpAU/women-of-ubisoft-lisa-pendse.

Metacritic. "Just Dance 4." Accessed September 2, 2020. Distributed by The Internet Archive Wayback Machine. https://web.archive.org/web/20121218040940/http://www.metacritic.com/game/playstation-3/just-dance-4.

Morton, Andy. "Anheuser-Busch InBev's Bud Light to Sponsor eSports League." Just Drinks, May 2, 2019. https://www.just-drinks.com/news/anheuser-busch-inbevs-bud-light-to-sponsor-esports-league_id128371.aspx.

Morton, Andy. "Dr Pepper Snapple Group Dives Deeper into E-Sports with Team Tie-Up." Just Drinks, January 22, 2018. https://www.just-drinks.com/news/dr-pepper-snapple-group-dives-deeper-into-e-sports-with-team-tie-up_id124970.aspx.

Nihon Keizai Shinbun. "任天堂・岩田社長が語る"本当の"ソーシャルゲーム" [Nintendo's President Iwata Talks about a "Real" Social Game]. Nikkei, January 6, 2013. https://www.nikkei.com/article/DGXZZO50298050V00C13A1000000/?df=2.

Pendse, Lisa. Twitter Post. May 18, 2020. https://twitter.com/MonaLisaPen/status/1262416282844114953.

Statista. "Teen Online Vs. In Person Gaming Frequency in the U.S. 2015." August 6, 2015. https://www.statista.com/statistics/454330/teen-online-and-in-person-gaming-frequency-usa/.

Quantic Dream. "Quantic Dream & Me - Interview with Lisa, Vice President of Marketing." February 27, 2020. https://blog.quanticdream.com/quantic-dream-me-interview-with-lisa-vice-president-of-marketing/.

CHAPTER 18: SEAN BAPTISTE

Markiplier. "1 Vs 1,000,000 | Doom Eternal - Part 1." March 20, 2020. Video, 1:26:49. https://www.youtube.com/watch?v=D8G-z5zJja3w&list=PL3tRBEVWohiAZqBxoGOgDi2IEUAiejw8D.

CHAPTER 19: MISSKYLIEE

Keng, Cameron. "Online Streaming and Professional Gaming Is a $300,000 Career Choice." *Forbes,* April 21, 2014. https://www.forbes.com/sites/cameronkeng/2014/04/21/online-streaming-professional-gaming-is-a-300000-career-choice/.

MissKyliee. "About MissKyliee." Accessed September 4, 2020. https://misskyliee.com/about-me/.

Miss Kyliee. "24 Hour AFSP Charity Stream." June 17, 2015. Video, 22:18.

Twitch. "How to Subscribe." Amazon. Accessed September 4, 2020. https://help.twitch.tv/s/article/how-to-subscribe?language=en_US.

CHAPTER 20: THESPUDHUNTER

Littledinamit. "Doom Eternal Rips and Tears Through Competition, Sells Over 700K on Steam." PlayTracker, March 29, 2020. https://playtracker.net/insight/posts/doom-eternal-steam-sales.

Minsker, Evan. "Nine Inch Nails' 1996 *Quake* Soundtrack Gets First-Ever Vinyl Release." Pitchfork, September 17, 2020. https://pitchfork.com/news/nine-inch-nails-1996-quake-soundtrack-gets-first-ever-vinyl-releaseandnbsp/.

Roses, Jonny. "Conquer Ultra Nightmare With This In-Depth Guide." Bethesda Softworks, April 17, 2020. https://slayersclub.bethesda.net/en/article/698ixOtkfQuuhkwFzp2tQC/ultra-nightmare-guide.

Stewart, Samuel. "Doom Games In Order." GamingScan, July 12, 2020. https://www.gamingscan.com/doom-games-in-order/.

TheSpudHunter. "Ultra Nightmare Guide and Tips for Doom Eternal." April 6, 2020. Video, 20:54. https://www.youtube.com/watch?v=jqaHMGhGzGE&feature=emb_title.

TheSpudHunter. YouTube Channel. Accessed September 21, 2020. https://www.youtube.com/channel/UCodDQd-JtN5kIfH4-A5L8UKg.

CONCLUSION

Statista. "Lifetime Global Unit Sales of Video Game Consoles As of September 2020." Accessed October 1, 2020. https://www.statista.com/statistics/268966/total-number-of-game-consoles-sold-worldwide-by-console-type/.